WALKING AFRAID

A Woman's Journey from Fear, Hurt, and Rejection to Faith, Wisdom, and Triumph

Carnela Renée Hill

Walking Afraid

Trilogy Christian Publishers A Wholly Owned Subsidiary of Trinity Broadcasting Network

2442 Michelle Drive Tustin, CA 92780

Copyright © 2024 by Carnela Renée Hill

Scripture quotations marked AMP are taken from the Amplified® Bible (AMP), Copyright © 2015 by The Lockman Foundation. Used by permission. www.lockman.org. Scripture quotations marked ERV are taken from the Easy-to-Read Version of the Bible, copyright © 2006 by Bible League International. Scripture quotations marked ESV are taken from the ESV® Bible (The Holy Bible, English Standard Version®), copyright © 2001 by Crossway Bibles, a publishing ministry of Good News Publishers. ©All rights reserved. Scripture quotations marked NIV are taken from the Holy Bible, New International Version®, NIV®. Copyright © 1973, 1978, 1984, 2011 by Biblica, Inc.™ Used by permission of Zondervan. All rights reserved worldwide. www.zondervan.com. The "NIV" and "New International Version" are trademarks registered in the United States Patent and Trademark Office by Biblica, Inc.™ Scripture quotations marked KJV are taken from the King James Version of the Bible. Public domain.

No part of this book may be reproduced, stored in a retrieval system, or transmitted by any means without written permission from the author. All rights reserved. Printed in the USA.

Rights Department, 2442 Michelle Drive, Tustin, CA 92780.

Trilogy Christian Publishing/TBN and colophon are trademarks of Trinity Broadcasting Network.

For information about special discounts for bulk purchases, please contact Trilogy Christian Publishing.

Trilogy Disclaimer: The views and content expressed in this book are those of the author and may not necessarily reflect the views and doctrine of Trilogy Christian Publishing or the Trinity Broadcasting Network.

10 9 8 7 6 5 4 3 2 1

Library of Congress Cataloging-in-Publication Data is available.

ISBN: 979-8-89041-497-7

E-ISBN: 979-8-89041-498-4

ENDORSEMENTS

This book is filled with so much wisdom! The first time I read it, I was so excited. Carnela shows you that pain and failure can STILL lead you to WISDOM AND SUCCESS!! (Duchess McKnight, Author & Speaker)

A mutual friend introduced me to Carnela over 20 years ago when she decided to pursue an MBA. Carnela always has a big vision for her future, and she has always been willing to take a degree of risk to move towards her dreams. I know that her faith has been a source of strength for her as she faced the normal entrepreneurship challenges along with the normal curve balls that life throws at you. One of the things I most admire about Carnela is her healthy view of failure. I believe that this perspective frees her to grasp and create opportunities for herself. (Katie Gailes, Creative Force at Katie Gailes, Inc.)

Carnela is an exceptional interior designer. Her attention to detail is the hallmark of her reputation. Consequently, this has garnered her a number of jobs with highly esteemed persons of notoriety. We have watched her grow and press through on her journey. Her story will be a blessing to others. (Bishop JJ Wilkins and Lady Cheryl Wilkins)

To reach the author for speaking engagements and workshops, visit her website at www.carnelareneehill.com

TABLE OF CONTENTS

Dedication 9
Acknowledgments 11
Foreword 13
Introduction 15
A – Amazing God 19
B – Better and Better 21
C – Confronting The Past 27
D – Determination, Disappointment, and Discernment 31
E – Empowered to Excel 35
F – Forgiveness 39
G – God, What Are You Doing? 45
H – Hidden in Plain Sight 49
I – Issue of Blood 53
J – Judgment and Jealousy 55
K – Knocking 57
L – Learning to Trust the Process 59
M – Mindset of Making It 61
N – No Means NO! 63
O – Open to God's Will 67
P – Peace Overcomes Guilt and Shame 71
Q – Questioning God 75
R – Relationships and Rejection 79

S – Successful Servant 83
T – Triumph at the White House 85
U – Under God's Covering 89
V – Vulnerable 91
W – Wisdom 95
X – X-Ing Out Fear 97
Y – Yes Is Coming 101
Z – Zealous for God 105
Now I Know 107
Walking Afraid Action Book 113

DEDICATION

Carnela dedicates this book to the life and legacy of Ms. Andrea Harris. You will forever live in my heart. You were a trailblazer for minority economic development on Durham's Black Wall Street, across the business world, and for entrepreneurs like me and many community leaders. The business world will never be the same because of you, for you left an indelible mark on all of us. I know you are smiling down and telling us all off at the same time, for we still have so much work to do. Thank you for challenging me and telling me to speak up. Rest in peace, Momma Andrea Harris.

ACKNOWLEDGMENTS

I dedicate *Walking Afraid* to my family and extended family, to the prayer warriors who prayed me through and did not always know why they were praying: When the chapters were tough to relive and my emotions were all over the place . . . when I could not pray for myself . . . you texted, called, and pushed me through. Thank you to everyone who challenged me, inspired me, encouraged me, and put up with me during this journey.

Thank you to my mom for always being there, yet letting me go so I could grow. To my Charlotte family, Tony and Jackie, thank you for letting me hide out and rest when I was tired. I am very grateful. Thank you to my sister from another mother, Timbuktu, and to my little brother, Gzee, who read a chapter and said, "Now we can talk." Thank you to my dads, Colvyn Gene and Rudolph; my other siblings, Patrick (Beatrice), Toia (Eric), Navares, and Nya; nieces, nephews, great-nephews, and other family members, for loving me unconditionally, supporting me, and putting up with me. Thank you for allowing me to be me!

To Bishop J. Jasper Wilkins and Lady Cheryl Wilkins, my former Wake Chapel Church family, and the other church families I visit on breaks (you all know who you are), thank you for allowing me to tear up your carpet. You will always have me as a designer.

Thank you to my sister friends, Shari and Monique, for your sisterhood and friendship. You truly have been there for me through the years.

Thank you to my sister, Janie, for making that call to ask specific questions, not understanding what you were doing; to my dear sister and friend, Sonya, for your faithfulness, support, and reminder to rest and maintain balance; and my other beautiful Ladies of Elegance sisters for your love and laughter. If not for my membership into the Gamma Beta Omega chapter, I would not have had the opportunity to be a part of the Chi Rho Omega chapter, so I celebrate all my sisters of Alpha Kappa Alpha Sorority, Inc. Thank you for letting me step away to put this book together while still cheering me on. And thank you to a special sister, Linda Henry, for submitting my name as an Emerging Leader and doing what you do in the community and for Alpha Kappa Alpha Sorority, Inc. I truly love and appreciate you!

To my BigMa and BigDaddy, continue to rest in heaven. You taught me so much! Thank you for being my grandparents! To my other family members who have transitioned from this life, including my sister, I wish we could have talked before you left. I love and miss each of you.

And to my secret weapons, LaMonique and Dr. Larue Coats: You are fierce, and I could not have gotten through the edits without you and your yellow highlights and red pens.

Carnela is no longer a member of the Alpha Kappa Alpha Sorority, Inc. Carnela has renounced and denounced the organization.

FOREWORD

When I met Carnela Renée Hill, she was modest, reticent, and reserved. It took a bit of being in her presence and a minor push to learn just how powerful she is.

I knew her as an entrepreneur who was an interior decorator. I assumed she dealt with residential clients. But this sister was bad: a North Carolina A&T computer science graduate with a master's degree from UNC—Chapel Hill Kenan Flagler School of Business, and a residential and *commercial* interior designer.

Soon I got to experience the wonder that is Carnela within a small group of African American female entrepreneurs who came together on a regular basis to learn together and be supportive of one another.

It soon became clear that, given her industry, she needed to be around architects and engineers engaged in the new construction or renovation of commercial and education facilities, estate housing, or small business design and renovation. Although her heart was with this group of women, Carnela realized the need to network in other arenas.

Carnela can be very focused, as one would expect from a programmer, but she is also quite humble. I still do not know if this sister realizes how good she is or recognizes the value of her work. You know you have made a difference when others see your results and feel good about what they see. However, when Carnela completes a job, she is happy for a moment, but then she starts to list the things she could have done differently. Meanwhile, I am just happy for her and in awe of her work.

On the occasions I have called or sent an email to promote and encourage an opportunity for Carnela to showcase her talent, she would do a wonderful job!

Never has she disappointed.

In the past, I had to encourage Carnela to speak up for herself in expressing interest in projects or opportunities in which she wanted to take part and to make the call. It baffled me why she was afraid and what she was afraid of. Now, she asks for what she wants and is confident in her God-given talents and ability to be a blessing to her clients.

Although fear is an emotion with which many of us struggle, Carnela has absolutely no need to be afraid, for she is truly a phenomenal woman doing extraordinary things! I know that her journey, like her work, will be a blessing to all within its reach.

—Andrea Harris, President Emeritus
NC Institute of Minority Economic Development

INTRODUCTION

I am excited and grateful to share a portion of my life with you. I hope my story encourages you to *walk afraid*, understanding you may know the Bible, but are you feeling secure enough to trust the process? We must stand on the promises of God, knowing He loved us before He created us.

My heart's desire for this book is to inspire, motivate, and push you into your next level, to make you look at the areas of your life you may have previously brushed over. I hope to make you rethink tests that reappeared to see if you have really forgiven the person. My goal is to help you seek God in a way like never before, to help you see the distractions before they come, and to immediately say, "God, You've got this. I've been here before, and I ain't going back."

I admit sometimes the annoying little voices of doubt creep in, contradicting everything God promised. Even as I was writing this book, distractions, fear, frustration, and doubt plagued me. There were times when I questioned what was going on.

"God, my God, what have I done? What do I need to do? I know You are purging me and strengthening me to be greater, but when and for how long?"

The tears would roll down my face, and then I would see an encouraging word, receive a call or text, and seek prayer. Some days, none of those things would occur, and I simply had to encourage myself. I would play worship music to keep my spirit renewed because I was tired and worn down. But I knew better than to give the enemy too much credit.

You may have prayed and slayed for everyone else, and you are asking when it is going to be your turn. We are human, and it is okay to be true to yourself and God, because He already knows what you are thinking. Keep giving God all the joy, the glory, the honor, and the praise.

I can write about fear because I have felt it. It shows up when I least expect or want it. I am telling you, just like I am telling myself, we must never be a slave to it again. God did not bring us this far to leave us, and we cannot let the enemy tear us apart. We were made for greatness.

My prayer is that you will keep pressing forward! Through decorating at the White House, eighteen years in a business that has had its ups and downs, health issues, relationships, rejections, and answering the call, I have had to press forward. I declare today that we will never again be a victim to fear. I release it every time it rears its ugly head.

Webster's Dictionary defines *fear* as "an unpleasant emotion caused by the belief that someone or something is dangerous, likely to cause pain, or a threat." God shows us in the Bible that fear is simply not trusting Him and not exercising our faith. His Word states in 2 Timothy 1:7: "For God hath not given us the spirit of fear; but of power, and of love, and of a sound mind."

Writing this book was not easy. I had to relive some challenging moments, like having a negative bank account balance, taking out a bad business loan, and watching people walk out of my life. Emotions surfaced that I did not realize were hidden in me. The new things that came out stretched me even more, so I could write this book and tell you that when you answer God's call, "It is well."

I am still smiling, trusting, and thanking God that He continues to walk with me, even when I do not seek His wisdom, guidance, and direction as much as I should. He chose me, and I have accepted His will.

Grab your erasable pen or pencil, and let's dig in.

> "I leave you peace. It is my own peace I give you. I give you peace in a different way than the world does. So don't be troubled. Don't be afraid."
>
> —John 14:27 ERV

More
Opportunities
Rising Everywhere

—Prophet Johnathan Brown

A - AMAZING GOD

For years, I lived in fear because of my past hurts, disappointments, frustrations, and general *stuff*. As my faith in God has increased, I have grown stronger in many areas of my life. I have developed a stronger core—with more peace, a stronger faith, and the ability to relax in Him. Even when I do not understand, I trust God's process and remind myself that God has never left me nor forsaken me. If God did it before, surely He can do it again! He's the *same God*! He changes not! When I do not see anything happening, He is still performing miracles on my behalf. I must *expect* miracles and favor! I have asked God to build me up where I am weak and help me not to become bitter and angry.

I remember dating a young man in college. I thought we would be together forever. He said I needed to be stronger because I was overly sensitive. In so many words, he felt I was weak. Yes, I knew that was an excuse, and I vowed not to let that happen again. I began to develop a tough exterior in relationships and work. I was determined never to allow anyone to call me "weak" again. Over time, I developed a hard shell, and I built a wall high to prevent me from getting hurt again. God eventually showed me it was hindering me from moving forward. That wall caused hurt in my personal relationships. I asked God to help me recognize when it was okay to let the wall down. Not everyone is privileged to get into my space.

Seek God for discernment so you can grow to another level. Forgiveness is necessary for you. There are times in life when the constant pain can be so intense that you struggle to let your guard down. You do not want to trust another person only to be disappointed. If we stay in that place, however, we will be stuck for life. God, in His *awesome* wisdom and power, knows how much we can bear. God knows everything about us. Yes, everything!

> *"But the very hairs of your head are all numbered."*
> —Matthew 10:30 KJV

God knows how much is too much. That is why God is so awesome, all-knowing, and all-powerful! If we had to rely on our own strength, we would be at the same place in life, dealing with the same mess over and over.

Aren't you glad God loves us so much that He is concerned about what we are concerned about? Trust that the people God places in your life serve a divine purpose! Ask God to teach you how to love again so you can receive everything He has for you.

I am looking forward to marrying the man God has for me. Because of God's awesome, divine power, I have been healed! I am whole! That does not mean the fear of being disappointed again does not cross my mind. It just means I have an answer and a Healer who mends my brokenness and places me back on the right path. I am consistent in asking, seeking, and praying for God's divine wisdom so that I do not keep making the same mistakes.

Life Lessons:
— Because God is amazing, He can turn your brokenness into wholeness if you are willing to trust Him and let go.
— Acknowledge your past and seek God for wisdom.

B - BETTER AND BETTER

I never saw it coming. I started my business part-time in January 2000, and I completed my MBA in September of the same year. Then I purchased my second new construction home. Things were going well, and I could not have been happier. I was steadily moving up the corporate ladder. I was on my way to another level in management. By 2005, I had moved into a new department. Then the news came down that the company was going through a major layoff period.

My vice president stated that everyone would be notified if they were going to be let go. I did not think anything of it at the time.

The Monday of the announcement, I had a doctor's appointment, so I had planned to work from home. When I got home from the doctor and tried to log in, I could not get access. But this was nothing new. After several attempts, I packed my bags and headed there. On the way there, my vice president called, asking me to call her in the New Jersey office when I got in. She told me my assignment was being terminated and I was being laid off. Thankfully, I had another opportunity within the company with another unit. I was told the layoff had nothing to do with my work or skills, but management felt the two company employees in North Carolina could easily find jobs because we lived in the high-tech RTP area.

Little did the executives know that another company in the region, Nortel, had just laid off thousands of people as well. Many of my friends were searching for jobs.

After prayer and clarity, God directed me to start my own business, full-time, instead of taking the job in the same company.

I was told by the unit director that I was very smart to take the layoff package and make the leap into entrepreneurship because everyone in the company might soon be searching for a job. God had a plan that was greater than me. I legalized and started the business full-time with the money from my severance package.

Six months after being laid off, I received a call to return to the company as a contractor, making even more money. It was amazing, and I still had my benefits for a short while. I also was offered a job to teach business classes at a community college, so I had income chasing me down. Once the contract ended a year later, I was able to return to working full-time in my business and teaching part-time. Remember, God's ways are not like our ways.

I was doing well work-wise, but I was suffering with fibroids, and they became a major issue. I felt like the woman with the issue of blood in the Bible. I was mentally and physically tired.

I had spent my 401K on the business and trying to sustain myself. I had marketing bills and medical bills piling up.

I asked God, "What do You want me to do?" I heard the Lord's voice clearly: "Sell the house. It has become a burden." I looked around the room to see if I had really heard God's voice, but I knew I had. It had to have been ordained by God, because the house sold within one day of placing it on the market, and many household items sold, as well.

Even after selling the house, however, I was having major financial issues because the housing market was plummeting, so fewer people were hiring interior decorators. A friend suggested I file for bankruptcy. I was angry at that suggestion because I did not want to face reality, but I was fooling myself. I was really struggling. After speaking to three attorneys, I finally filed for bankruptcy. The attorney said I was paying everyone except myself. He submitted a mandate for me to relinquish the business, as well as a truck that was dying, and all my bills. I cried and cried. I felt like a failure. I think the stress of it all caused the fibroids to worsen.

I reopened another design business with a new strategy. I had no time to be fearful. I felt I was wearing a big *F* on my chest. No one really knew except the people closest to me, but I felt like the entire world knew.

Many times, we carry guilt and shame that others do not see, and it is a heavy burden to carry. A friend reminded me that entrepreneurship is not for everyone. It takes strength, determination, perseverance, and faith the size of a mustard seed. So, I got my new business in place with a new strategy, with no marketing and hopefully less pain. Business was slowly picking up, but it still was not that great.

The fibroids in my body continued to be an issue. I was placed on temporary medication and had frequent doctor visits to help with the pain and bleeding, but it was not working. The smell of gasoline and, at times, food made me nauseated. Some days were unbearable, but I did not have time to stop.

In the midst of this turmoil, God blessed me with a huge opportunity to be the designer for a church—for free. I asked, "Lord did You really tell me to do this pro bono? Really? Do You see my bank account? God, I am struggling. My corporate job is gone, I have sold my house, and entrepreneurship is not what it is cracked up to be." However, I was obedient, and God continued to keep me and bless me!

About six months later, I ended up in the hospital, because I just could not keep food down. I was in excruciating pain. I could not even sit or stand. The doctor said he needed to operate immediately because the fibroids were growing. The doctor was surprised that I was still able to move around.

I bled for most of that summer with little relief. If I took just a sip of water, my bladder would fill up. I was miserable. I was beginning to eat pain pills like food, and I had no energy. It was only by the grace of God that I was still standing. I told the doctor I needed to wait on the surgery until after I finished summer school because I also was in the middle of the big pro-bono project. So, I finished teaching summer school, and then I had the surgery.

With the surgery and bankruptcy finally behind me, I worked to reestablish myself and my new business name. It was hard to obtain any type of loan because of my previous bankruptcy. Seven years passed before the doors once again opened for me, and I had to wait eight years for the bankruptcy to completely clear from my credit history.

I felt that every time I got close to obtaining a business loan, roadblocks with large barricades were glaring at me. I thought that surely decorating at the White House would make things better, but traditional lenders told me my business had grown too fast. It was a great problem to have, but it prevented me from moving forward with the business.

Yes, my business had grown quickly, but I knew that playing in the arena with the big boys meant I had to have cash on hand. My numbers looked good on paper, the clientele was there, but the steady cash flow was not.

Most small business owners understand this fluctuation. I worked hard to build a business, sacrificing my needs for my business and the team, and it started to feel like a burden instead of enjoyment. I had to change my mindset and seek God for answers. I asked the Lord for wisdom and a business strategy. So many nights and days, I cried out, "Lord, help Your daughter. I need You!"

Just when I was starting to feel defeated, it happened. The clients I prayed for and who were meant for me started calling. God sent people of influence to help and guide me, and doors began to open all around me.

Do not get me wrong, I still had other issues, but I had a team of resources and knowledge from other successful business owners to guide me and to share their stories. I am usually the one to pour into others and provide insight and wisdom, so I was thankful to have the right people to begin to pour into and direct me. That's God's way!

Still, I had to learn to be strong and watch the people who were coming to be helpful. I realized that not everyone who smiles in your face is always in your corner. At one point, I ended up taking out a loan that was not a wise fit for me. I take full responsibility for my actions, but it taught me a great lesson. If it sounds too good to be true with a few red flags, *stop!* Remember, for every "no," there is a "yes" waiting to happen. Just make sure the "yes" is from God.

During this time, I saw people shift, and God gave me clarity. I quickly learned that who is with you for the short term may not be who is with you for the long term. I realized that when people discounted me, it made me step up my game and give it all I had. I know what God has promised! I will walk in what God has promised for my life. Not everyone can go with you!

Some people are only with you for a short while. Once they fulfill their mission or you fulfill yours, they are released from your life. Count it all joy and keep moving forward!

Life Lessons:
— You are not alone—no matter what, God is with you.
— Ask for big things and expect *big* things!
— Keep pouring out. Your living is not in vain!
— For every "no," trust God for His "yes"!
— Some people only serve a short time and purpose in your life; do not stop their departure. Your next steps and your growth may not include them.

C - CONFRONTING THE PAST

I have had to confront many areas of my past that have caused me fear and heartache. But doing so has challenged and strengthened me for the next part of my journey. The fear of rejection was a major ongoing issue in my life, and I realized I had to understand the root of the rejection in order to move forward.

I had to deal with my biological father not being fully in my life during my childhood. I never thought the lack of a relationship with my father would have such an impact, but I can see now that my bitterness was building. Over the past six years, I have had to ask myself some hard questions and work to forgive him.

Once I grew up and started working in the corporate sector, I saw firsthand the judgment and prejudice at each of the three companies in which I worked. My first corporate job, after college, placed me on a management track. For one of my assignments, I worked on a project with a white female manager who did not work well with African American women. The manager critiqued and judged my work in ways that were demeaning. I was young and determined to climb the corporate ladder, so I did not fully understand what was occurring. I had great mentors at the job who pulled me aside and explained to me what was happening. I was crushed.

So, I went to my safe spaces—church, the Bible, and counseling. Subsequently, I was moved into another department, and my new manager had no clue how the previous manager could have described me in such a negative way in conversations and in my file. I had to work very hard to prove to everyone that the previous manager was wrong. I was twenty-three years old at the time, and I was very disappointed.

Shortly thereafter, the company went through a layoff period. Because I was the newest hire in my new department, I was first in the layoff lineup. The new manager cried when she told me she had to lay me off because she knew all I had experienced with the previous manager. I was just starting to overcome everything I had been through when the layoff happened, so I was stunned that I was being let go.

I prepared for the next opportunity by spending the next two months finding a new job. I received an offer with an IT company, and I thought I was set, even though I knew the job would not be long-term because the company did not have a growth plan. The person who referred me told me I was too talented to be in the position for very long, so I kept that thought in mind.

I had gained some telecom programming experience in my last job, and it prepared me for the new position. I have learned that God will prepare you for what is to come even when you do not understand why you are going through what you go through.

The new company was getting a new telecom system that I was familiar with, so I moved into that area. I was even asked by my male supervisor to train others in the department. After I completed the initial training for a male co-worker, the company began promoting from within, and I discovered by accident that the gentleman I had trained was being promoted over me. I saw a new organizational chart with his name above mine. The good ol' boy network was evident. Even worse, I had to continue to train him.

This man was also sexually harassing me. He was married but constantly asking me out and making sexual remarks that were not appropriate. He knew I was dating someone, but he did not care.

When he was promoted, his remarks grew stronger. I was under so much stress that I tried to avoid working late. I never complained because I did not think the supervisor would believe me. I had already seen how the men at this company viewed women. I was eager to leave.

Again, I went deep into the Bible for clarity, and I immediately started looking for another job. Not only was there limited growth at the company, but it was also clear I would not be considered for the few opportunities available. I did not need the headache anymore, and the stress was making me physically and emotionally sick. I was ready to release the stress.

Now I regret not reporting the incidents. I have the same sexual harassment story as so many others who have come forth due to the #MeToo movement. I did, however, tell a close friend about it so I could release it.

You do not have to be afraid, and you do not have to deal with this, especially in the workplace. I pray no one else experiences what I did. I urge you not to allow anyone to take your peace. Neither general harassment nor sexual harassment is acceptable. We do not have to live in fear of what might happen if we report it or what might happen if we do not accept a predator's advances. Do not allow guilt or shame to keep you from moving forward. You are unique, and Jesus paid everything for our sins. You are stronger than you think, so do not shrink back.

I found out later that the administrator asked my supervisor to at least speak to me about the new organizational chart before it came out, but he refused. He did not even respect me enough to have the conversation.

The door was closed. I needed to walk through it. I resigned and moved on to the third telecom company. I was placed on the fast track, things were going well, and I was promoted several times. I worked for a white male supervisor who was bothered that the executives would call me to assist with special projects. The executives held quarterly Diversity, Equity, and Inclusion (DEI) conference calls, and if I was not on the call, they would summon me or ask me to follow up. The supervisor incorrectly felt I was "brownnosing" when the executives called on me. It created an uncomfortable work environment in which I was unduly scrutinized.

I never fell behind on my work, and I actually excelled, but the supervisor held my relationship with the executives against me. That supervisor moved to another department, but the incoming supervisor was a teammate who allowed her friendship with the previous supervisor to hinder a fair assessment of me. Eventually, I moved to another department and was promoted shortly thereafter. Finally, I left the company altogether and started my own business full-time.

Dealing with rejection, racism, and prejudice was hard to manage in my twenties and early thirties. As I look back, however, God prepared me for each job, and my faith grew every time. I now see how my past and working in the corporate sector shaped my future and my current business.

Depend on the Lord. Trust in him, and he will help you.

—Psalm 37:5 erv

Life Lessons:
— There is purpose in pain. Healing will happen!
— What was meant to kill you only makes you better.
— Change how you look at a bad situation and see the lesson therein.

D - DETERMINATION, DISAPPOINTMENT, AND DISCERNMENT

What happens when you wait on God? Every time I have waited on God, He has blown my mind! With waiting comes so many things. As I waited to purchase my SUV, my old SUV was slowly transitioning to vehicle heaven. Several people shared with me that it was time to get a new SUV. I wanted to hear from God myself, because I did not want to go ahead of God's plan, and I have not had a car payment in five years. My old car had 327,000 miles on it and was going downhill. I called her "Black Beauty." She had been a beauty at one point, but she had lost her luster all around. I test-drove more than ten cars in my quest to replace Black Beauty. I knew exactly what I wanted, and the price needed to be amazing. Approval was very difficult because of my self-employment status, but finally, I was approved. I had 180 days to find a car, or I would need to be reapproved.

I thought this task would be pretty easy, but it proved to be very difficult. I was becoming frustrated and asked God whether I should wait. I did not know what was going on. I found cars out of state, but it was a headache to get them, and the bank might not have approved the transaction. One of the dealerships hit the "all" button to get me a cheaper interest rate, and I ended up with more than fifteen hits on my credit report. Still, I tried not to grow weary.

Eventually, I found a car out of state. The owner agreed to drive it down for the bank's approval, and I would drive to Pennsylvania the week before to check it out. The day before I was supposed to go to Pennsylvania with a good friend, I got the feeling things were shifting. My friend could not drive with me, and no one else was available. This car was the right price, with low mileage and an extended warranty, but it was from a private seller. I was distraught, and I began to question God and everything. It appeared that every time I went after something, I was thrust into so much opposition. Family members and friends said I wanted too much in a car. Why did I need all the extras on this car? God had to work on me with disappointment. But I knew I would have the car for years, just like my old car, and so I wanted all the bells and whistles. However, I started to think my family and friends were right, and I began to decrease my list of wants.

Then one day as I was driving, I saw my car. I knew this was my SUV. It appeared to have everything I wanted and more. I went through the process with less than twenty days before my approval ran out. It was clear. I had been looking for a 2013 vehicle to keep my payment down, but I heard God say He was upgrading me.

The vehicle I had spotted was white with a two-toned interior and was loaded with all the features I wanted—and more. The dealership let me drive it for a little more than seven days as I waited for the down payment to come in. I would return the car during the waiting process because delays were all around me, but the dealership would repeatedly send me home with the car.

To my surprise, the down payment was almost four thousand dollars. I asked, "Lord, what is going on?" The finance guys could not work the deal, my funds were not coming in quickly enough, and just like that, the car was sold out from under me. Through it all, I kept saying, "Jehovah Jireh, You are my Provider."

I was back in my old car, and it was putt-putting along. I was spending so much money on the old car just to keep it running. I had stopped looking so hard because it was such a task.

I finally saw a car online with all the features I wanted, except it was gray, but the price was about the same as the white one. I went back and forth, and then the price dropped by four thousand dollars. *Yes!* When I called the dealership, God had already orchestrated everything. A nice lady named Ashe answered, and the ball began to roll. Everything she asked me for, there was a delay on my end and her end. She could not understand what was going on. I began to pray and call my prayer warriors, my close circle of friends and family members who know the power of prayer. Little did I know, Ashe was praying also. By the end of that day, she sent an email that said, "Come get your blessing!" I did not see her message because I was trying to pull together the other documents, so she called and asked if I saw her email. We rejoiced together!

That same morning, prior to speaking with Ashe, I had prayed, "God, I need You like never before in every area of my life." Sitting in my old car, I began to cry out. I could not go into my office. I had the urge to make a desperate plea for God to shift my life financially. That same day, one of my biggest clients called to say that the date I'd put on my invoice would delay the receipt of my payment and for me to resend the invoice with the date change so that I would receive the check more quickly. Yes, *Jehovah Jireh* is my Provider! He is the Way Maker!

> *In all the work you are given, do the best you can. Work as though you are working for the Lord, not any earthly master. Remember that you will receive your reward from the Lord, who will give you what he promised his people. Yes, you are serving Christ. He is your real Master.*
>
> —Colossians 3:23–24 ERV

Life Lessons:
— Learn to *wait* with expectancy.
— Wait with a grateful heart and the right spirit. God is watching your responses to situations.
— Let God's voice overpower the other voices. When delay comes—and it will—ask God to reveal to you the lesson you are supposed to learn. God used the car situation to grow me. I am grateful. It was never about the car; it was all about the life lessons.

E – EMPOWERED TO EXCEL

I am excited about the many wonderful things God is bringing forth. I am learning how to best tell my story. Friends are getting their radio shows, and the atmosphere is changing. I asked a good friend, Jimmy D, the visionary and mastermind behind Every.Black Entrepreneur Network, about a radio spot. He chuckled and said, "I thought about you, but the shows are geared toward entrepreneurs. I do not see an interior designer in the mix." I shared the inspirational and motivational work I had been doing and that I wanted to do more inspirational work on a large platform. He said he would see.

I received a phone call two days later, on a Friday afternoon. Jimmy D, the visionary, had good news. "Yes, I got you a show. I did not call you for your acceptance. The radio executive asked if I wanted to check with you and I said no . . . she will do it." Jimmy went on to say I would be the co-host of an inspirational and motivational show with national comedian and glamour girl Kimberly Vaughn. I said to myself, *How is this going to work with a comedian?* Truly, God has a sense of humor, and perhaps God thought I needed to improve mine. I always joked that in my next life, I would become a comedian. Kimberly was in Missouri, and I am in North Carolina. I did not know her, but she was working on a TV show and was out on a motivational tour. Since I believe in the motto that God will place you in the company of kings and queens, I felt it was my season. My time had come, and I was going forth. I had also been working to secure a TV show, but I had just received the news that the show was not going to happen. Still, I knew there was a show coming with my name on it. When God closes one door, He has the ability to open another!

Kimberly and I tried to start the process, but our individual schedules were tight. We eventually recorded our first show, and it was good. So was our second show. Then, as oftentimes happens when we think something is good, the atmosphere shifted. The show was about to be cancelled. Then, God did what He does best. Bishop Bates, the owner of 88.1 The Truth Network, and Kimberly and Jimmy D talked. Kimberly moved on to prepare for another show, and the universe opened for me to have my own show. God can and will blow your mind when you least expect it, so stay ready!

"Empowering You to Excel" was birthed, and I was the host. I was having the time of my life. I started preparing, and Jimmy D sent me the marketing materials he had prepared for the show. I was once again blown away. The cover was a huge bird, and the encouraging scripture that Jimmy had chosen for me was the following:

> *"Have I not commanded you? Be strong and courageous. Do not be frightened [or afraid], and do not be dismayed, for the L*ORD *your God is with you wherever you go."*
>
> —Joshua 1:9 ESV

I believe that you have not because you ask not. God spoke and continues to speak to me about asking *big*. Now, I have opened myself up to voicing *ginormous* requests, and not just miracles, signs, and wonders are evident, but mind-blowing prayers are being answered! My heavenly Father holds the key to all things, and my life is in *His* hands. God will make all things new! God is a WayMaker! Have you seen God make a way in your life?

God is a Promise Keeper. Even if it does not look like anything is happening, God is turning things around for His glory. Take God at *His* Word and stand on His promises that it shall come to pass in His due time.

God is not a man, that he should lie; neither the son of man, that he should repent: hath he said, and shall he not do it? or hath he spoken, and shall he not make it good?

—Numbers 23:19 KJV

Life Lessons:
— There is nothing too hard or impossible for God. If God said it, then it is done.
— Do not give up on your dream. Praise God through the storm and the distractions.
— A dream deferred is not a dream denied.
— A delay is not a denial. Seek God for the next step.
— God can turn water into wine and make two fish and five loaves of bread feed thousands. Trust Him to change your situation.

F - FORGIVENESS

God's Word and voice has been so profound to me in some areas, but not as loud in others. The great thing is that through it all, I knew God was always with me! I have learned to pray before I enter business contracts and friendships. The fear of repeating past mistakes has opened my eyes. Yes, when you begin to have relationship issues—be they personal, business, or with your family—you must start to ask what you are supposed to learn and what you could do better. I have had clients whom I would never have suspected bring craziness and drama into my business. Every time one hurdle passed, there was something else lurking. I just threw my hands up and said, "Daddy God, let this cup pass."

> *Abba, Father, all things are possible unto thee; take away this cup from me: nevertheless not what I will, but what thou wilt.*
>
> —Mark 14:36 KJV

Friday, January 20, 2017, started out as an ordinary day. I was living in a new year and a new season of my life. New beginnings! School had started, and I was in a very good place in my life with a new mindset and peace. But that afternoon, I was in an accident that changed my life.

I went to school that day and decided to meet a client-sister-friend for dinner. We agreed to meet at Homegoods first to see what was new and from there head to dinner. I had to make a stop at the mall before driving over. I traveled about four miles, and the traffic was getting heavy. I was the first person at the light, waiting for it to change, and then I heard the loudest *bang* imaginable. There was a tap on my window, followed by apologies. In my mind, I heard my little nephew's voice saying, "Not today."

I pulled over to the side of the road with the gentleman who had hit my car. That one moment changed the rest of my year. I began to have aggravated pain in my body—in my head, neck, back, and buttocks. Many of my normal tasks were altered due to the pain.

I wanted to make sense of this. I was trying to understand what happened, but I could not. A few months after the accident, I participated in a mastermind-style business call, but instead of the usual group, only ladies were on the call. I heard God say, "Pray." I asked the ladies if I could. What a revelation it was for the three of us on the phone, including me!

At that moment, I understood the purpose of the accident. God allows things to happen so He can get the glory! One of the ladies on the call said, "The accident was meant to take you out. Do you understand that? But you have a greater purpose that you must accomplish!" This was just a distraction—a painful one—but God never said there would not be some pain. I mean pain with a capital *P*. We all left that call feeling free!

I have grown so much from the accident. I forgave the driver. I pray continuously for his job and family because, as I checked my car and his, I kept hearing from God, "This man has a family." One year of consistent pain and altering daily tasks is frustrating, but when you understand your purpose and calling, you learn to pray and press through the pain. The accident could have ended badly, because I was the first car at the light and the traffic on the cross street was moving fast. The driver had been drinking. I am so grateful for the hand of God on my life. I had to keep forgiving, especially when the pain got stronger; I had to keep learning to trust God's process and let go when instructed.

One time, a person whom I thought was a friend did things behind my back, and God warned me, but I was still trying to see the good. I was afraid I was going to miss out on business from my carnal eye, but the Spirit was warning me. It was loud and clear: *If you do not back away and shut it down, it will be detrimental.* God reminded me that my friends are not my source, and my clients are not my source: He is my only true Source! God sees all and knows all, and I do not need to rely on people, but rather trust in Him. Now, that was not easy! Again, *the devil/fear comes to steal, kill, and destroy.*

I was being disobedient, so if I stayed by choice, the "consequences would be detrimental." When God warns us, sometimes it is a soft message, and other times it is hard. We have free will. No friendship or business is worth our disobedience to God. Sometimes we do not realize how disobedient we are being.

When the relationships around you are in upheaval, *stop* and listen. A lesson is likely contained in the message. Relationships can be crazy, but family relationships can be worse. You still have to see them, deal with them, and love them at family functions. You want to scream, "Why me, Lord? Why me!" But you already know why—you were chosen! They do not think you know what you know. They are a part of your assignment, and they just keep trying your patience.

At some point in time, hopefully sooner rather than later, you will need to *let it go*, continue to pray for them, and watch God work. Yes, I have a few in my family whom God has made a part of my assignment. At times, I am so afraid that if they do not get in line with God's will, it is going to be detrimental to their lives.

God reminds me that I cannot take on everyone's battles and that I must stay in my lane. I know you want the best for your family and friends, but God's Word says:

> *For my yoke is easy, and my burden is light.*
>
> —Matthew 11:30 KJV

God reminds me that my assignment for family members and certain people is to pray first, to seek Him to reveal what He is saying, to be a listening ear or to provide guidance. It is important to understand that you can be obedient in your assignment while not taking on any of that person's mess or stuff as your own burden. Lighten your load and weights.

Assignments appear in many ways, including in jobs, from employees, in school, and with people you barely know but to whom God directs you to deliver a message. I have been in jobs and leadership positions that I have loved initially, only to become frustrated at the end. We have all been there. You loved what you were doing or the people, but you disliked all the other stuff, including the background noise, the not-so-nice people, and the darts constantly being thrown at you. Or you are disappointed when a boss tells you that they would choose another person over you if it came down to making a decision, even though the other person is wrong, and the boss knows it. Stay encouraged!

God may still tell you to stay because you are on an assignment. He sees all and knows all. I wish I had learned some lessons early on in life. God may tell you that a certain person is your assignment for the season you are in that job or role, and you must pray for that person, regardless of how they treat you. "Really, God? I still have to work at this job and deal with this stuff?" The answer was, "Yes, and God, strengthen me through the process."

So many times, we want to run from the very thing that can bless us and catapult us into the next level God has for us, because we allow people and things to stand in our way. It is easy to say you trust the Lord with all your might, but when you are put to the test and a myriad of things are coming at you, do you trust God enough to remain obedient?

When God directs you to share a word with someone, it can sometimes be difficult to be obedient because you wonder if they will think you are crazy. When God directs you, make a wise decision to go forth. I would rather be a fool for God and be used by Him than to be disobedient to the Lord. You never know the life you will save or the blessing and breakthrough that will be linked to your obedience. God can simply lead you down a certain street or to a store that could help someone or bless you. Be obedient to the Word of God, for obedience is better than sacrifice.

> *The fear of the LORD prolongeth days: but the years of the wicked shall be shortened.*
>
> —Proverbs 10:27 KJV

> *The LORD All-Powerful is the one you should fear. He is the one you should respect. He is the one who should frighten you.*
>
> —Isaiah 8:13 ERV

Life Lessons:
— Do not let FEAR (False Evidence Appearing Real) hinder God's plan.
— Obedience is better than sacrifice.
— God honors our sacrifice when our heart is right.
— Serve the Lord with fear and trembling (Psalm 2:11).
— Forgiveness is not always about the other person. When you forgive, you free *yourself*.

G – GOD, WHAT ARE YOU DOING?

It's my winning season! My life is changing in every area! God is speaking, and things are happening. This is a winning season. I am enjoying my new ride. My life is changing all around. Business is flourishing, and things are happening.

In fewer than thirty days of owning the car, still praising God for favor, I was returning from dinner one day when I came face-to-face with a huge deer. It was as if the deer decided to stand in the street. I swerved to keep from hitting her, and she just took her tail and hit the front right bumper of my car. I was so dumbfounded and shaken that one of my sister friends had to check the damage. I was less than two minutes from my house. I got home still in awe of what just took place and grateful it was not worse. In thirty-two years of driving, I had never hit or been hit by a deer.

The next morning, I got up to go check my car, convinced the incident was a bad dream. But nope. I had hit a deer. God reminded me it could have been so much worse. I almost hit the deer in the middle of the car instead of the rear. The deer did not crash through the windshield. It was just a distraction. *Keep moving!* I got over it, paid the one-thousand-dollar deductible (what in the world?), and all was well.

That was a busy week. I had to attend a conference in Las Vegas, and I was ready to learn. I breathed a sigh of relief when I got on the plane and said, "Okay, God, I do not know what You are going to do in the next four days with this conference, but I am open. *Blow my mind!*"

On Day 1, I had a light-bulb moment, but still I needed more. The change of time zones was affecting me, and I was getting tired.

On Day 2, the phone rang early for both the Pacific and Eastern Time Zones. The installer on one of my design projects needed to check something before the kitchen installation. Then my design assistant called. I was getting ready for my training, and I was already tired before the day even started because there was so much going on. I was almost numb. Then, I had another *Aha!*—a light-bulb moment. I had so much work to do, but I was moving forward. God gave me peace that everything would be okay. I knew there was a purpose for this trip. I went expecting the unexpected, a move from God.

On Day 3, I was praying for some things to be released and a mighty move of God to occur. My meditation was on point this particular morning. The early-morning phone calls were still occurring, with my assistant letting me know the client's alarm was going off and the client was not happy. I was tired and had had very little sleep because my conference roommate locked herself out of the hotel room. Fast-forward, and I was preparing for the conference that day. I prayed for everyone there, for a release from distractions and fakes in the room, for relief from the strongholds to be broken from the day before, and for a shift in the room. That morning was simply amazing! God shifted me to walk in my gift. I received confirmation from one of the conference attendees/ministers. She explained that I was struggling with my gift of ministry and my gift of design, and that I could not be afraid of ministry. Yep, extremely clear! That day, I was hearing God like never before! God amazed me at the conference—and the entire room! God moved in me to be a blessing. I praised God and came back with a new perspective!

A day later, I attended a CD release event for one of the ministers at church. I left the church and was about two minutes from the house when I saw the car near me swerve. I swerved also, and *bam!* No, not again . . . Another deer! I held the steering wheel so tightly, blown away by what had just happened.

Lord, another deer? Really? Now, this deer was bold. He actually tried to ride with me. Glass and deer-coat fibers were everywhere. The back and third-row seats were covered with glass and deer hair. The rear passenger window was blown out, and the frame of the window was cracked and broken. I called the insurance company—another one-thousand-dollar deductible. I still needed to pay my insurance for the month. *Help me, Lord!* I sat on the floor of the house, too distraught to cry.

The next day, God provided for me to pay the insurance. I called the insurance company, and they told me I was a month ahead on my payment. They asked if I wanted to pay ahead or have it refunded back. "Refund it back!" I said. *Thank You, Lord. You heard my cry again!*

Another week passed, and I headed to church driving the rental vehicle. I was about to turn into the parking lot, when two deer ran across the church parking lot in front of the car and then into the woods. I screamed, "Lord!" I was driving with my mom on the phone, and she jokingly responded, "Maybe they are leaving the meeting you are attending." My prayer partner suggested I look up the significance of "deer." There it was in plain sight:

> *He maketh my feet like hinds' feet, and setteth me upon my high places.*
>
> —Psalm 18:33 KJV

I can truly say God got my attention! For a while, I was afraid to drive in desolate places, and I began to fear driving at night, not that deer are not bold during the day. God made it clear that the deer accidents were a distraction, and the best was yet to come! The tension, stress, and pain of the ordeal felt like more than I could bear. But God took care of the deductible. More importantly, God has taken care of *me*. My fear of deer will not paralyze me.

Don't worry about anything, but pray and ask God for everything you need, always giving thanks for what you have. And because you belong to Christ Jesus, God's peace will stand guard over all your thoughts and feelings. His peace can do this far better than our human minds.

—Philippians 4:5–7 ERV

Life Lessons:
— Be still and know that He is God; listen for God's still, small voice.
— Things happen; do not dwell on what you cannot control.
— Discernment is a blessing.

H – HIDDEN IN PLAIN SIGHT

Have you ever been searching for something, like your keys or wallet, but could not find it? When you finally stopped to ask for guidance, God would lead you to it, and you see it was in your face the whole time, hidden in plain sight.

It has been prophesied, and I have heard God say, "You have been hidden in plain sight, but now I am about to really expose you to the world." Yes, to that positive exposure! "People thought it was something to see you go to the White House, but what I am about to do next is going to blow even your mind!"

Hearing this made me so excited, and I anticipated the "Big Reveal"! Yet, at the same time, the opposition swings hard and causes distractions.

This time is not for backing down, no matter how hard it gets. This time is for standing flatfooted, to throw back your head and command what God has said. Bishop Neil C. Ellis, presiding bishop of Global United Fellowship, says that you must decide if you are going to run with the horses or stay with the footman. If you are running with the horses, then remember, a horse sleeps while standing on all four legs.

> *"Jeremiah, if running in a race against men makes you tired, how will you race against horses? If you trip and fall in a safe place, what will you do in a dangerous place? What will you do in the thornbushes that grow along the Jordan River?"*
>
> —Jeremiah 12:5 ERV

I have decided to run with the horses. I have learned to press my way through.

For I have learned to be content whatever the circumstances. I know what it is to be in need, and I know what it is to have plenty. I have learned the secret of being content in any and every situation, whether well fed or hungry, whether living in plenty or in want. I can do all this through him who gives me strength.

—Philippians 4:11b–13 NIV

There have been times when I have been looking for items as I was working on a design project. When I am in design mode, if I do not seek God, I am all over the place. Recently, I was looking for a large container. I had been to two stores and to one of those stores twice. I asked the store manager to call or check to see if the items were at the other store before driving thirty minutes to get there, and she checked haphazardly, with an attitude, as if I was bothering her. It was a good reminder to watch my own attitude because you never know who is watching you. As I went to the third store, I searched and searched. I found one of the containers, slanted and charcoal-gray. Yes! I felt in my spirit that the other container was there. I continued to search, and then I heard God say, "Look up!" There it was—the container I had searched for. I was reminded, "Hidden in plain sight, like you!"

When God is about to bring you out, you will feel like your world is crumbling, but just before it does, the sky will open, and God will blow your mind! God is building your faith and testimony. I look up more now because all my help comes from the Lord. Looking down only makes my neck hurt. Looking up acknowledges the Lord and His sovereignty.

Before the test you must take, there are many distractions. During the test, the distractions are even greater. Remember, the teacher is often quiet when you are taking the test. However, after you pass the test, there is a celebration! Do whatever it takes to pass this test. Do not get caught up in the distractions; it is all part of the process. The reward is greater after you have made it through. My sister friend Kenya said it best: "You cannot go higher without the stretching!"

You are not defeated. You are an overcomer. *This is your winning season!*

Life Lessons:
— You have been hidden in plain sight for God to reveal who you are in His timing.
— Stay focused on God's Word.
— Do not get caught up in distractions.
— The process is necessary.
— Chaos is sometimes necessary; it often has a purpose.
— Remember the Big Reveal.
— You are running with the horses, not the footman.

I - ISSUE OF BLOOD

And a woman having an issue of blood twelve years, which had spent all her living upon physicians, neither could be healed of any, came behind him, and touched the border of his garment: and immediately her issue of blood stanched.

—Luke 8:43 KJV

In 2007, I felt just like the woman with the issue of blood. I was dealing with repeated surgeries from fibroids, and this particular year was the worst ever. I had a menstrual cycle almost every day for an entire summer. My cycle would go off for a few hours or a day, then it would come back on. I was mentally and physically drained. I could not keep food on my stomach. I could not get comfortable sitting or standing. At the time, I did not have health insurance. I had just sold my house. I was teaching during the summer and also working on a huge project. I decided to go to the hospital emergency room because I was hurting so bad. A friend said it just might be indigestion, but I knew it was more. I could barely get out of the car at the emergency room because the pain was so severe in my stomach and side. After I was wheeled into the hospital, the doctor started the process of determining what was occurring. My pain was an eleven on a scale of one to ten, and the pain medicine was not working. The only issue the doctor could see was the fibroids. As I got X-rays, my bladder kept filling up. The X-ray technician was amazed because I would empty my bladder, and it would fill right back up. The doctor said I needed to have surgery. I was referred to an ob-gyn, who confirmed I needed to have surgery as soon as possible. I was the woman with the issue of blood, and I needed God to take this away.

The summer school quarter would last two more weeks, but my doctor said it was not advisable for me to continue with the level of pain and the bleeding I was experiencing. I was concerned about everyone else but myself. I was concerned about the church project, about my students, and about my clients. Meanwhile, my very health was in jeopardy. Finally, I had to stop and have the surgery. God has a way of making us rest when we do not know how to sit down on our own. I was forced to rest for two weeks, but it was necessary for me to work my gift. Just like the woman with the issue of blood, I wanted to be made whole. I was tired of the hormonal changes, and I had spent a lot of money to get a resolution. I needed a different outcome.

Life Lessons:
— Take care of *you* first.
— Do not sacrifice your health to the point of neglect.
— Take the time to rest and listen to your body.
— Let God's desire to make you whole be more important to you than your desire to just be healed.

J – JUDGMENT AND JEALOUSY

Chances are, you've experienced judgment or jealousy at some point in your life. You have likely felt the sting of someone's judgment or envy. Perhaps you were even the one judging another person or situation, or maybe you were jealous about what you saw as someone else's blessing.

There is only one true Judge over all the earth. I know I can be very critical of myself, so I do not need anyone else onboard judging my every move.

Sometimes judging myself has blocked God's blessing. Now I ask God to send what I need and show me how to receive what He is saying. Do not let the naysayers (including you) keep you from God's best. Do not let the naysayers talk you out of your blessing or out of God's promises and plan for your life. Ask God to help you silence the noise that is coming at you.

> *For it is the will of God that by doing right you may silence (muzzle, gag) the [culpable] ignorance and irresponsible criticisms of foolish people.*
>
> —1 Peter 2:15 AMP

Ask God to give you discernment. Seek God for wisdom so you may hear His voice over all other voices. A person who is jealous or envious typically shows his/her hand to you before it is obvious who he/she really is, so you must pay attention to the signs and believe it the first time.

God has allowed me to see the enemy in a dream or hear them clearly in a face-to-face encounter. I know, we all want to believe the best about people. However, it is better to learn the lesson early on and stop any foolishness. When I have missed the signs, God has sent warnings and made it clear to stop and seek Him for wisdom and guidance! We are all a mess, so aren't you glad for redemption and deliverance! God has saved me from myself. Yes, won't *He* do it!

If you have been the envious and jealous one, it is time to check yourself. I have asked God to help me deal with the spirit of envy and jealousy so that I can be delivered. God will show you where your motives are self-absorbed and sabotaging all He desires for you. He will show you where purging needs to occur.

Thank You, Lord, for purging me! Make me new and make me whole.

Hatred stirreth up strifes: but love covereth all sins.

—Proverbs 10:12 KJV

Create in me a clean heart, O God, and renew a right and steadfast spirit within me.

—Psalm 51:10 AMP

Aren't you grateful God gives us another chance to get it right? I am not perfect, but I strive to serve the perfect One every day.

Life Lessons:
— Ask the Lord to cleanse you and make you whole.
— Ask the Lord to take you and your mess, and make you into His masterpiece.
— Only the Lord can judge you.
— Ask the Lord to forgive you for participating in gossip and judgment.
— Ask the Lord to remove envy and jealousy so you may operate fully in His divine will.

K - KNOCKING

Are you tired of running from God? Are you tired of bumping your head against the same walls? Have you had the same dreams over and over, but you have not done anything toward truly understanding them because you know God is asking you to do things in a different way from how you are accustomed?

Yep, I can relate. I have had repeated dreams of me speaking or preparing to speak/preach. I either wake up or never make it to where I am supposed to go onstage. Then, there are repeated dreams of the doorbell ringing. I have gotten up, and there is no one at the door and no signs of anyone ever being there. I have had dreams of knocking at the door, opening it, and seeing myself standing on the other side. For me, this has been the repeated dream and sign of God's calling on my life.

What is so amazing is that God gives us ample opportunities to answer His call, but most of the time we ignore it. We choose not to acknowledge it. I have been guilty of this inaction. I said, "Not me. God is not calling me like that." However, if God is calling you, please stop ignoring the call.

> *Therefore, Eli said unto Samuel, Go, lie down: and it shall be, if he call thee, that thou shalt say, Speak, Lord; for thy servant heareth. So Samuel went and lay down in his place. And the Lord came, and stood, and called as at other times, Samuel, Samuel. Then Samuel answered, Speak; for thy servant heareth.*
>
> —1 Samuel 3:9–10 KJV

I have chosen to answer the call. My call may be different from yours. Only you and God know what He has asked you to do.

Even if you are walking afraid into your calling, continue to walk. Once I realized this design business was not mine—that my home, my car, even my life, was not my own, that I own nothing, and I owe God everything—then things began to change. You may have had some success prior to truly understanding Who is Boss, but not to the magnitude of what God has in store for you.

God gives us a good measure of success. Obedience and following God's plan open doors that we cannot fathom. No one is righteous or perfect, but we must strive for perfection and delight in His ways to obtain the success He has in store for us.

When I design in myself, I am all across the board and struggle to make decisions. I waste time and money, making decisions that cause me to stop and think. However, when I ask God to take control, the project *blows my mind*, and the peace and harmony that come into the space are unimaginable.

I am still learning lessons. I have not *arrived*. I am learning to open myself up more and more to His will and His ways. As I do that, He stretches me beyond my wildest dreams. The stretching has not been easy, but it has been absolutely worth it. The process is necessary! I am seeking the greatest prize, and that is to hear Him say, *"Well done, thou good and faithful servant: thou hast been faithful over a few things, I will make thee ruler over many things"* (Matthew 25:21 KJV).

Life Lessons:
— The more you study and meditate on the Word of God, the more you will build your spiritual life to hear God's voice.
— Stop fighting the process! If God has called you to do a task, give it your all. Show that you expect God to deliver on His promises by delivering on yours.
— Seek God for clarity and direction. It is okay to walk afraid—just trust that, in due time, God will give you understanding.

L - LEARNING TO TRUST THE PROCESS

Faith is the substance of things hoped for, the evidence of things not seen.

—Hebrews 11:1 KJV

Tell God your plans, and you will quickly learn His plans. In the past, I have trusted man instead of trusting the warning signs from God. After bumping my head over and over again, I have accepted that if I am to obtain a different outcome, I have to do things differently. If you expect differently, you must do differently! If God is growing you and maturing you to another level, your old ways of doing things will not work.

Then you hear God's voice. It could be to wait, trust, turn down this street, or go down this path. When God speaks, sometimes the answer and His guidance are different from what you expected.

My sheep hear my voice, and I know them, and they follow me.

—John 10:27 KJV

Recently, I was dealing with a client situation. I did the work, sent the invoice, and got no response. I sent the invoice again, and the client told me he needed more information and floor plan options. What I had provided was more than sufficient. This situation began to wear me down physically and mentally. My team and I had put a lot of time into completing those plans. From our conversations, I had believed the client and I were on the same page. We had met with the client, and he had been happy. Now this!

I prayed, but did I wait to hear the answer? Did I do my part? No, I did not. But I thank God for another chance to get it right.

I reached out to the individual. The responses were slow, and then the responses went cold. I kept asking God what I should do. I heard God say, "Wait, I've got this!" I began to complain and become frustrated. I had to release this distraction every time it came to my mind, and that was often.

About two weeks later, with no response, I received a phone call from the general contractor inquiring about the job's status. Shortly thereafter, I received a phone call from the client. God was letting me know that He was working on it. He needed me to trust Him with it all. God was sending signs all around me. Even during the process, I had to ask God to take my mind off the situation. I was becoming too obsessed with the disappointment and frustration. I was mad at myself because I did not sign a contract. I had trusted the person because of the title. Just when I gave it back to God and left it in His hands, I received a call. I never received the hard-earned money that I had worked for, but I learned a lesson. Put your trust in God. Do the follow-up work, and God will do what He does in His time and His way regardless of the outcome. You will learn a lesson or be used for a lesson. God is waiting on you to *trust Him* and have *faith* in His *process!* Once you move your feet, He will provide all you need to move forward.

> *Do not forsake wisdom, and she will protect you; love her, and she will watch over you. . . . Though it cost all you have, get understanding.*
>
> —Proverbs 4:6–7b NIV

Life Lessons:
— Put your trust in God only.
— Wait for God to give you an answer!
— Stop talking and listen.

M - MINDSET OF MAKING IT

With any change, you cannot keep doing the same thing and expecting a different outcome. You must change your mind and your actions. Change how you think. You must surround yourself with positive people and people who push you to the next level.

Surround yourself with people who are moving forward. Seek discernment, and pray about everything. Trust God like never before!

You will have days when you want to give up, throw in the towel, and shut the world out, but you cannot do that. You cannot give up. You must keep pressing forward. Your "greater time" is coming! The change you seek is based upon your faith—faith the size of a mustard seed. I know it is hard to stand still with the earth moving around you. I understand and know the feeling. This Scripture puts things in perspective:

> *"Everyone to whom much was given, of him much will be required."*
>
> —Luke 12:48b ESV

So, how bad do you really want it? I will admit, there have been times when my faith has not been what it should be. I just wanted to throw in the towel. But I remembered all God has done. I remembered that if He brought me out before, then He will bring me out again. The fact that He woke me up this morning should be more than enough. The fact that He walks with me and carries me when I am tired, weak, and frustrated should be enough. The fact that He has taken my mess and created a masterpiece, even when I was not-so-good, should be enough. He keeps on making a way!

Create in me a clean heart, O God; and renew a right spirit within me.

—Psalm 51:10 KJV

You are not alone in being afraid to take that next step into something new, like entrepreneurship, ministry, or a new job that may pay less than your current one but is divinely ordered. I have had anxious thoughts, experienced the utilities being turned off, had a car repossessed, and nearly lost my house to foreclosure in pursuit of a dream that others only see as glamorous. Some people are only with you during the glory, yet they disappear when it gets hard. They are not there when you cry all night asking God to help you through the sickness, the debtors calling, and the wondering when your time was coming. At times, life happened, and I could not tell anyone for fear of being judged, ridiculed, or told to go get a "real" job. Not everyone will understand the dream God put in you!

If God told you to do it, then you have to do it, even if you are afraid. Even if the storms are looming around you, know that God will give you the peace that surpasses all understanding to let you know you are on the right track.

Now faith is the substance of things hoped for, the evidence of things not seen.

—Hebrews 11:1 KJV

Life Lessons:
— Trust God more than yourself and man.
— When it gets hard—and it will—stay in constant communication with God.
— Remind God of His promises to you.
— Keep writing the vision and making it plain.
— Let God direct your path.
— There is nothing too hard for God.

N - NO MEANS NO!

No more cancer.

No to an old boyfriend who is drunk and takes advantage of you.

No to the demands of life and people pulling on you.

No to needing approval with likes, hearts, and smiley faces.

No, no, no!

No is acceptable. *No* is not just a word—it is also a statement.

No more cancer!

Recently, my mom went to the doctor. The doctor said she was a miracle because she has been cancer-free for more than forty years. *No more cancer!* My mom said, "By the grace of God, I am healed!"

What are you believing for this day? If God can do it for my mom and heal her from cervical cancer, I know He can do it for you. By His stripes, you are healed.

For there is no respect of persons with God.

—Romans 2:11 KJV

No Means No

I went out on a date with a friend, a past boyfriend. Everything was good, and we were having a good time. He had a drink or two, and I did not think that was an issue. We went back to his place to watch a movie, and he had another drink. Before I could grasp what was happening, "no" became a repeated plea of my words falling on his deaf ears.

It has been more than twenty-five years, but I finally had to come to grips with the trauma of that night when the person started reaching out to me. I was in a state of letting go of the old in preparation for the new. I was letting go and forgiving old boyfriends and relationships. God was breaking soul ties and strongholds. I was in a place where I wanted to prepare for the husband God had promised, so cleansing from past relationships was bringing out a lot of hidden mess.

I confronted him and reminded him of that night. He remembered and apologized repeatedly. He said he wondered why I stopped reaching out to him over the years and did not return his calls. Through that conversation, I was set free, and so was he. I thought I had forgiven him a long time ago, but now I can truly say I have.

No to People Pulling on You

Are you the one whom everyone calls when they need help, but you can barely find a person when you need it? Are you the family member, friend and/or coworker who struggles with saying "no"? This is your moment to be set free. Deliverance is a beautiful and peaceful thing! Stop feeling guilty and shameful for saying "no." Stop committing and saying "yes" because you are being pressured. Self-care is a necessity when doing kingdom work. Put your mask on first.

My sorority sister Sonya is a poster child when it comes to "no." She constantly reminds me to say "**no**" and rest: "You do not have to do everything." After the car accident, she frequently texted me to say, "Are you resting?"

I used to feel so guilty about saying "no," but God has brought me into a new place where I can freely say "no" or "another time," if it is necessary. To write and finish this book, I had to say "no" to a lot of things. I am so glad I did!

No to Man's Approval

Perhaps you are in a place where your confidence and self-esteem are low, and you feel like you *need* approval with likes, hearts, and smiley faces. Social media can feel like a big popularity contest that will make you lose your mind. People will like you today and talk negatively about you tomorrow.

I ask God to help you (and me) on those days when we get caught up in what man is saying, and to remain constant, believing in the work of the Lord. We have all allowed people to dictate how we feel. However, we need the Lord more than we need likes, hearts, and smiley faces!

God, purge us of our old ways and make us brand-new in You, in the name of Jesus!

It is a rebirth to say "no" to cancer, "no" to depression, and "no" to needing likes, smiley faces, and hearts! Say "no" to foolishness and craziness! I am now very comfortable with repeating the word *no* with power and meaning. I want you to get comfortable with saying "no"!

Let's practice: *No, No, No, and heck no!* I'm sure we still have work to do, but my prayer is that you will allow "no" to flow when you need it.

Then, when the "yes" comes, you will be ready for it because you were able to rest and be restored, and you said "no" when you needed to do so.

Life Lessons:
— No!
— No, no, no!
— NO!
— Nope!

O - OPEN TO GOD'S WILL

In order to unlock the plans God has for your life, you must be open to His will. You must be willing to accept God's timing. Let me tell you, it is not easy.

> *For as the heavens are higher than the earth, so are my ways higher than your ways, and my thoughts than your thoughts.*
>
> —Isaiah 55:9 KJV

I am so glad God's ways are higher than my ways and that God does not hold a grudge, because I have been guilty of limiting God by what I think I can do. God specializes in the impossible! He can turn your situation around in the blink of an eye.

I have desired a godly husband for a long time—and not just a godly husband, but a committed, tall, dark, and handsome husband with a few characteristics that I do not have room to share in this book.

In my thirties, it was prophesied that God had a husband for me, but I kept encountering the wrong type of man. I knew then God had to do a work in me. I could keep dealing with the same old thing or be open to the one whom God sent, when He sent him, and how He sent him. If I chose to fight the process or be disobedient and take matters in my own hands when God finally revealed him and before God spoke to him or released us to come together, then I could delay the process. As God has been preparing me, it has been uncomfortable at times. Past relationships have left me hurt.

Marriage is a huge step. While some focus on the wedding day, I want longevity with my husband and soul mate, so I am willing to be prepared, pruned, and given away by the spiritual Father to the man He has handpicked for me when He says it is time. I want my king from the King of kings! I have made up my mind to be open to God's will and God's way.

In 2017, God was speaking to me about resting and about my health. My body was being greatly impacted by poor sleeping habits, bad food, and always being on the go. I would change for a short while and then go back to the same bad habits. I began to see the warning signs. My doctor warned me that if I did not get it together, I would have to take medicine for diabetes and high cholesterol. I was determined that this would not happen to me. I decided to take heed because I wanted to be around for my family, for my husband (whom God has promised), and for the fulfillment of the mission for my life. I no longer wanted to disappoint and be disobedient to my Daddy/Father God!

I had to give up my sweet tea; now I have only occasional chai tea lattes and chocolate-dipped madeleine cookies. A healthy, whole life or food—the decision was not as difficult as I made it out to be. I began the process before my car accident. After the accident, I had to start over. I got back on the horse and remained committed.

I lost the first five pounds and got comfortable. Then I became committed to the quest and lost another five pounds. I was on cloud nine because I had accomplished a huge task. I was down ten pounds! Still, I teetered and postponed my doctor's appointments. I saw a friend losing weight, and again I got back on track. I pushed myself and lost twenty pounds. What an amazing goal I had met!

Set the goal and stay focused. If you get off-track, just start over. After a while, you will get tired of starting over! You will also realize that whatever you truly want in life requires giving up something or somebody. To receive that which we want, we must be dedicated to the end more than we are to the beginning.

Life Lessons:
— If it did not work your way before, try God's way. He can never fail!
— Great things are worth the wait.
— If you quit before the end, you can always start over! Force yourself to stay committed to the end.
— Let God's perfect will be done.

P - PEACE OVERCOMES GUILT AND SHAME

I have made some bad choices in life that have caused me to feel embarrassed and ashamed. For years, I avoided talking about my bankruptcy because I was embarrassed. I was embarrassed about my financial situation. I stopped talking about my health issues because people started labeling me as sickly and always suffering in ways that did not appear ordinary. Some things I caused myself, and other things I allowed to happen to me. God blocked some things, but He allowed others, so He could get the glory.

I was attending a women's conference, and I was not in a great mood. I was dealing with the fibroids, my funds were low, and I was fighting to keep my business open during the economic downturn in the housing market. I felt like a failure. My spirit was as low as it could be, but I had to keep my sanity. I continued to believe God and trust His Word, although I was having a bout of unbelief. In my desperation to hear from the Lord and be around other believers, I attended the women's conference. It was just what I needed.

If you are fighting to attend a worship service, for whatever reason, understand that most likely you are supposed to be there, because God has something special for you. When I have truly dreaded going, God has delivered a miraculous word.

At the conference, the prophetess spoke, and I was set free. She shared that I had been embarrassed. She told me, "God wants you to tell your story. No more guilt, no more shame, and no more condemnation. Your story will bless others. The tears were part of God's cleansing."

I do believe that everything I went through was for such a time as this—the rape by a drunk friend that I held in my heart for years . . . the police ride downtown for a $3.75 bounced check . . . selling my dream house before the bankruptcy and having to stay with family and friends to continue working the business in the area . . . the continuous issue of fibroids causing my hormones to be out of whack and the bout of depression. It was all necessary.

I was lonely, although I was surrounded by people. I refused to take the medication for depression. It made me crazy. I flushed it down the toilet and stood instead on the promises of God that could not fail. I compromised my beliefs and damaged my spirit by living with a boyfriend without the benefit of marriage, and the guilt plagued me.

I am so grateful to have the freedom to talk about all this. God has been better to you and me than we can ever thank Him for! God is amazing; I mean, He is *absolutely amazing!* The guilt and shame can no longer paralyze me.

Casting all your care upon him; for he careth for you.

—1 Peter 5:7 KJV

Release that guilt, that burden, that feeling of failure, because you are *victorious*! No one can tell your story like you. It is your story. You went through the pain and hurt, and only you can tell it! Believe it or not, you are much better now. God has wiped your tears and your past away. God has renewed and restored you. Once you release your past, you have been made whole and set free!

Thank You, Lord, for healing our brokenness and making us brand-new in You. We receive a fresh anointing and know You will never put more on us than we can handle. In Jesus' name, amen!

And the peace of God, which passeth all understanding, shall keep your hearts and minds through Christ Jesus.

—Philippians 4:7 KJV

Life Lessons:
— Nothing is too hard for God!
— Even in your pruning, you are a blessing.
— Tell your story and free yourself.
— You are not crazy. What you went through was real, and do not let anyone tell you differently. Seek God to keep moving and growing into the best you ever!

Q - QUESTIONING GOD

Have there been times in your life when you have wanted to ask God:
- Why?
- Lord, how long?
- What is going on?
- When, Lord?
- No, not now?
- I thought you said you would not put more on me than I can bear?

You seek God for answers. You ask questions that you were taught never to ask. You do not understand, yet you know God does not make mistakes. Your heart hurts. You want an answer!

God is not a man, that he should lie; neither the son of man, that he should repent: hath he said, and shall he not do it? or hath he spoken, and shall he not make it good?

—Numbers 23:19 KJV

When my grandmother, affectionately called BigMa, died, I was somewhat prepared, yet it still hurt. She made me sit down with her six months prior to her death to discuss money, what to do for her service (although everything was laid out, even down to her clothes and casket), and how to help my mom through it. I remember not wanting to have that conversation. She told me I could handle it. It would be hard on my mom, but I could handle it.

BigMa was ready to go! At the time we had our talk, she was in fairly good health and loved serving the Lord. When she passed away on Wednesday, March 30, 2005, I had to step up.

I was reminded of growing up and not being able to hang out with other young people because she was preparing me. A boyfriend came over to the house with shorts on and did not open the door for me. She pulled him to the side and told him, "Those legs are pretty, but you are never to disrespect a young lady and come here with your legs showing." From that day, no matter how hot it got outside, he wore his shorts over but went to the side of the house to put his slacks on before he rang the doorbell. And he never got in the car again without opening my door first.

My BigMa treated everyone as if they were her child or grandchild. Yes, there were so many young people who came to visit her, and she babysat their children to help relieve the pressure of daycare on families. She had an amazing love. She shared wisdom like a running faucet, with love and humor. She was "old school," humorous but firm in her answers. Everyone who knew her and knew of her, knew she did not play around. She meant what she said and said what she meant with a heart of love.

After my BigMa passed away, I was in the airport headed to New Jersey. I met a prophetess who revealed to me why God had taken my BigMa home to be with Him. It was time. God had said we were too dependent on her. I accepted that answer, and now I understand more than I did years ago.

Yes, the family and I had depended upon my BigMa because she was the matriarch of the family. She was a wise and praying grandmother! The *why* now makes sense.

Sometimes the *why* will not make sense for a season, or even forever. It could be as simple as God saying, "Because I said so!" I am seeking God for the answers to a few things in my life right now. If He gives those answers now or never, the fact remains the same: I must trust Him.

I wanted children. I attach to them, and they attach to me. Early in life, I knew in my spirit I would not be able to have babies. This desire is one of those *why*s that I do not understand, but I have accepted God's will because there are so many kids who need someone to hug them and talk to them. God has given me so many nonbiological kids to love that I could never have a dull day! My nieces jokingly say, "Auntie Carnela spoils us for a short while, and then takes us back home at any time." These are wise kids! They know me too well.

God knows what we need and when we need it. God does not always give us the answer like we expect it. Actually, the answer or solution is often unlike what we have ever imagined. I am so grateful, and I hope you are, too! If God had come through when I wanted Him and how I expected it, I would have missed His greatness!

Life Lessons:
— He is an on-time God! Do not miss the blessing because you are blinded to your own way.
— Your greatest blessings look nothing like what you thought. Actually, none of your blessings have likely looked like you imagined!

R - RELATIONSHIPS AND REJECTION

That special one shows up, and you think that person will be the "husband/wife one," but after heartache and "hell-ache," you realize he/she is not and will never be "the one." You've got to be more careful! That pain runs so deep, and you are upset with yourself for allowing that mess to occur.

Yes, you were blind to that foolishness at times, but the warning signs were always there, and you just closed the shade. God gave you the warning the first, second, third, and fourth times to *let it go!* You were afraid to trust God and let it go when you knew in your spirit it was not right.

It is time to forgive them and yourself. They have already moved on, yet you are still allowing it to invade your space.

Maybe you have been hurt from a relationship with someone at church, and you have got to see them every Sunday. You want to confront the person, but God has told you to be still and let Him fight your battle. For a while, you struggle with releasing the matter, but then you give the hurt and pain back to God. Let me share with you that after a while, you will not be fazed by the situation, and the peace of God will overtake you!

When money is involved, it is often easier said than done to forgive and let go. However, God will give you double for your trouble. He will make it easy and put you in a place where the person who wronged you will have to speak/depend on you, and you will know God has shifted the atmosphere. God has heard you. He always hears you.

Sometimes rejection will come from people who are blatant about how they feel about you. You are valuable as long as it is beneficial to them. This is especially true when you are young and in a new field, organization, town, job, or church. What do you do? Realize that not everyone is going to like you, so just get over it. Do the right thing anyway by seeking discernment and moving forward! If people want to leave or do not like you, let them go. Stop trying to make people stay that do not want to.

Sometimes the people who hurt you are members of your own family. I have a wonderful family. Do not misunderstand me—all of us have our flaws. We do not always agree with each other or get along. In my family, I am the one who listens to everyone else's problems. But there are times when I must tune them out and not answer. I continue to be present for my family—after all, that is what family is for! But I have learned that I must take care of myself first. I am reminded that I must put on my oxygen mask before I can assist others. I have learned this lesson the hard way. Some family members have kept their distance because of this, but I am okay, because there is only one of me.

Life Lessons:
— You may have been hurt, used, and abused in past relationships, but still, forgiveness is a must.
— Do not stay stuck because you refuse to let go.
— Remember, each relationship, good or bad, prepares you for what comes next in your life or the one you must help.
— It is so true that some people are in your life for a season. You will know when that season may be up.
— Take care of you! *Let go* of the old.
— The more you give, the more people will expect you to give.
— You must determine whether you love you enough to say "no" when you mentally and physically cannot give anymore. Do not allow guilt to force you to give in.

— Hurt from those who are in the church can make you turn away from God. Do not allow it to cause you to lose your faith and your relationship with God!
— Check yourself. Sometimes it is *you*! Self-evaluation is a must.
— Stop trying to make old relationships fit into the new thing God is doing.

And no man putteth new wine into old bottles; else the new wine will burst the bottles, and be spilled, and the bottles shall perish.

—Luke 5:37 KJV

S - SUCCESSFUL SERVANT

Too often we look at society's definition of *success* as the acquisition of cars, houses, vacation homes, and name-brand items. I can relate, and I have had that same mindset before. Yes, God wants us to have nice things! However, there is more to life than these things. To be kept by the peace and favor of Jesus and to see your family blessed, healthy, whole and saved cannot be purchased. To be a blessing to others, freely giving, is a level of success that very few seek. Is this how you measure your success? Reality check!

According to *Webster's Dictionary*, *success* is defined as "the accomplishment of an aim or purpose." I have been told I was afraid of success. I thought, *Me, afraid of success? Hardly!* But I realized I have allowed fear to keep me from being successful. Yes . . . fear of another bankruptcy, fear of failure, fear of not being able to pay my employees. Once I recognized and acknowledged why I was fearful, I decided to let it go!

I have made a promise to myself that I will walk out this journey, despite my fears. When fear creeps in, whether it be of taking a test, purchasing a building, or walking into my calling, I will allow God to ease my pain and hand over the fear that has had me in a paralyzed state for too long. This is the time for me to walk into my destiny. This is our WINNING SEASON!

I seek a life of giving more without restrictions or guilt because of my bank account. I seek a life of traveling with my husband and enjoying my journey. I am getting better at my work-life balance. I enjoy getting in the car and driving over two hours to see my family. This is my quiet time, another time to talk to God.

Humble yourselves in the sight of the Lord, and he shall lift you up.

—James 4:10 KJV

This is what I deem as success. Do not get me wrong . . . extra cash would make it better. I desire enough money to live comfortably and to be able to be a blessing to others. I want more free days to do volunteer work, speak, mentor kids, and coach entrepreneurs. Lord, lead me to Your definition of *success*. I am so grateful for all God has allowed me to accomplish, and I cannot wait to see what He does next. I am sure it will be mind-blowing because that is just how God works. I am excited about the new work God has called me to do for His Kingdom! I encourage you to write down your own definition of *success*.

Life Lessons:
— Get a journal to write down the lessons you learn and to track your growth.
— Ask God for direction and listen for His answer, then move ahead based upon that answer.
— Ask God to send you a great prayer partner who will keep matters confidential.

T - TRIUMPH AT THE WHITE HOUSE

Many people do not know I applied to the White House before 2014. Although I did not receive a rejection letter, I was not accepted that year. That wore me down in spirit because I really wanted to go. I could have stayed stuck there and not bothered again, but I made the decision to trust God and let Him prepare me. I was not sure what that meant, but I put my petition before God.

When the next opportunity came, God went ahead of me and showed me the steps and the people who could help me prepare. There were roadblocks, distractions, and discouragement that came from other people, but God strengthened me. That is why you cannot speak too soon and to everyone about God's plan for your life—just keep preparing.

When I finally received good news, I checked my email at least four times to make sure I had read it correctly! Some of my discouragers were surprised. But remember, what is for you is for you, and it will come to pass.

In preparation, I was the coordinator of special events and decorations at my church. I put together a proposal for three large angel charity trees at the church for Christmas. We got three large trees and one small tree. The committee came together in mid-November, because I knew I would be leaving for the White House soon.

I rode the train to Washington, D.C., on Thanksgiving Day to decorate the White House. For most of my life, I have celebrated Thanksgiving with my family. My mom knew I was going, and I talked to two close friends on the train ride up. I became very sad, to the point of tears. A happy time became a sad time. I was missing my family and Thanksgiving dinner. But then I had a pep talk with myself. I called upon the One who had orchestrated everything, and peace fell over me. I was going to the White House to decorate! Take the wheel, God!

God gave me time to reflect and clear my head during this trip, to let go of pride and ask for help. I had very little money because I was waiting to be paid from a commercial project. Actually I needed God's help even to pay for the hotel. This was volunteer work, so you had to pay your own expenses. My family and friends pitched in and paid for my hotel room for seven nights, as well as the train ride and meals. I was worried every day about how I was going to pay for this trip. I did not want to tell my family or friends, but I was forced to ask for their help. God made it impossible for me to fail! You receive not because you ask not.

Fear could have kept me paralyzed, but I refused to allow it.

The thief cometh not, but for to steal, and to kill, and to destroy: I am come that they might have life, and that they might have it more abundantly.

—John 10:10 KJV

Is fear stealing, killing, or destroying your peace and joy to live abundantly? Stop allowing fear to control and manipulate you!

When I got to the White House, it was a beautiful experience. Again, God showed up and placed me on the right team, surrounded by the right people, and He worked His power. I was chosen with a few others to decorate the Oval Office. When your steps are ordered by the Lord, get ready for an explosion of blessings! I was then called upon to help with another room. Creativity kicked in, and God showed out!

Although I was happy and elated, I could not get fully joyful. The God on the inside kept me humble. I understood my assignment was bigger than just decorating. The attack on Paris happened in December 2014. Perhaps my assignment was to pray. I just hoped I fulfilled God's purpose at the White House at that appointed time!

When I finished my assignment, I took the train back to North Carolina. I shared the news with a few close friends. By the next morning, my Facebook page was blowing up. My fabulous PR manager, Jill, followed up with the interview requests. I was not even back to my house in Raleigh yet. I was still resting at my mom's house in my hometown of Wilson. I quickly sprang into action.

One of the happiest times of my life truly became a time of sadness, because ugly spirits came about from people whom I had thought were close friends. Again, I had to dig deep because my spirit was starting to wonder! I was reminded that when you are blessed to carry out an assignment, not everyone is happy for you. They will throw in your face what they did to help, but they will not acknowledge that you gave them their credit. Of course, this is nothing new, but God reminded me that He was in charge and this was a distraction. People were being weeded out who could not go with me to the next level. Just like I had served my purpose at the White House, they had served their purpose in my life. There is no bitterness or hatred. I have learned to love them regardless of how they feel. I know my heart was right, and God sees that.

Life Lessons:
— You will either choose to accept the shift or stay stuck. I chose to shift!
— Not everyone will be for you.
— Man's rejection is not God's rejection; a delay is not a denial.
— Discernment is a beautiful thing when you listen and let God lead you.
— You never know who is watching you. Always put your best foot forward.

Trust in the LORD *with all thine heart; and lean not unto thine own understanding. . . . It will be health to thy navel and marrow to thy bones.*

—Proverbs 3:5, 8 KJV

U - UNDER GOD'S COVERING

I grew up in a small town—Wilson, North Carolina—and I traveled around the country; joining the ranks of corporate America; making a six-figure salary; preparing for marriage; enduring BigMa and BigDaddy's passing; experiencing bankruptcy, several heartbreaks, four surgeries (including a hysterectomy that rendered me barren); becoming a campaign and fundraiser manager, a set director for a movie, and a decorator at the White House; navigating negative bank accounts; watching my mom survive cancer; hosting radio shows; writing this book; and now, walking in my divine calling. I had to stay under God's covering. God is good, and there is so much more to come!

Whenever something big is about to occur, the enemy does whatever possible to discourage, distract, and debilitate you so you will take your eyes off what God has for you. I serve notice, declare, and decree that this book will change lives as God intended! I trust and believe it will fulfill the mission and purpose God intended for those who read it. Everything the devil has told you is a lie. So, whose report will you believe? I believe the report of the Lord!

Right before the finish line of anything destined for greatness, rocks, bricks, boulders, and steel will be thrown at you. Whether you see what is coming or not, stand flatfooted and speak to every mountain. God did not make you a failure. You are *victorious*! You are a champion! Tell your story and keep it moving. You have the mindset of making it, and no devil in hell can stop you.

Under the covering and protection of God, we declare His promises over our lives. Repeat this affirmation to yourself:

I am no longer walking in fear. I am walking, running, and jumping into my destiny. My past is just that, my past. I will not dwell therein. I will seek wise counsel. I will give God my best. I am not defeated nor depleted. I am BLESSED! I am BLESSED! I am MORE BLESSED! What held me back before will not hold me back anymore. My bank account is overflowing, my hands are strong, and my Father sits on the throne! I have everything my Daddy promised, because He said He would not withhold any good thing from me. Not only am I speaking over my future, but I am declaring my present situation to line up with what God has intended for me. Everything must align with the will of God, even my thoughts and my ways. No more self-sabotaging actions. If God did it for Jabez, surely He can and will do it for me, as I set my mind and heart on Him. This is my prayer, my declaration—in Jesus' name, amen!

If you do not know the Lord, know that you can find safety in Him. Surrender your life to God and start attending a church of baptized believers who are walking with Jesus Christ!

I pray God's grace and favor over you, to give you the desires of your heart as you wait patiently for His timing.

No weapon that is formed against thee shall prosper; and every tongue that shall rise against thee in judgment thou shalt condemn. This is the heritage of the servants of the LORD, *and their righteousness is of me, saith the* LORD.

—Isaiah 54:17 KJV

Life Lessons:
— Today, tomorrow, this week, next week, this year, and in the years to come, I will continue to make it a point to **walk afraid**!
— Ask God to surround you with people who will cry with you, laugh with you, and grow with you.
— I am God's masterpiece, uniquely made! You are God's masterpiece, uniquely made!

V - VULNERABLE

I have had days when I did not want to go out or talk to anyone. The world of entrepreneurship can bring out emotions of loneliness, depression, and oppression, but I thank God for His grace and mercy for not allowing me to stay in that place. I am being so vulnerable right now, but I realize that if you continue to ignore feelings of depression and oppression, you will never heal and become your best self.

What is the difference between oppression and depression? *Oppression* is the state of being subject to unjust treatment or control, persecution, repression, suppression, and subjection. *Depression* is having feelings of severe self-doubt that turns to despondency and dejection, feelings of inadequacy and guilt, often accompanied by a lack of energy and disturbance of appetite and sleep.

Did you know the average entrepreneur is four times more likely to experience depression than others, according to psychologist Glen Moriarty.[1] Entrepreneurs are expected always to be strong and keep it moving, but sometimes you just want someone to listen without trying to solve your problem or you just want to cry it all out, wipe your nose, and go back to work. Yes, really!

According to a study by Dr. Michael Freeman of the University of California at San Francisco, one in three entrepreneurs live with depression, and 30 percent of all entrepreneurs experience depression, but most never tell anyone.[2] When your stress

---

1 B. Kerr, *Depression Among Entrepreneurs Is an Epidemic Nobody Is Talking About*, October 26, 2015. Retrieved from https://thehustle.co.
2 Ibid.

levels are up because you are always waiting for a check, you are struggling to make payroll, a small problem with a client turns into a major problem, or your dreams go up in flames from a bad business deal or taxes, it is easy to see how a person can become depressed. No more pretending or sugarcoating: Depression in entrepreneurship is real!

Entrepreneurship is not easy, but I would not change it. However, I would change some of my behaviors and my mindset. You must be resilient. You had better know how to pray an effectual prayer.

The effectual fervent prayer of a righteous man availeth much.

—James 5:16b KJV

Trust me, I am grateful. Any potential business owner needs to have a mindset of constantly seeking greater knowledge and save three times more money than he thinks he needs. Being a single entrepreneur is not impossible, but it requires commitment, faith, determination—and money. The struggle is real. If not for my faith, I would have lost it a long time ago. I would have surrendered my Boss Card for a nine-to-five job, but I thank God for the strength to keep moving. I know interior design is part of my ministry and the stepping-stone for many future blessings in my life.

Entrepreneurship is not for the faint of heart. If this is your path, then surround yourself with people who know you well and also know when you are *not* yourself. If you must get help, it is okay. Allow yourself time to heal and stay healthy.

You *can* be a successful entrepreneur. Keep God first. Pray about everything! Balance your life with non-work activities and enjoy time with your family. Stay passionate and do your work on purpose. If you are passionate about your purpose and purposeful in your passion, you will not allow anything or anyone to keep you from accomplishing your dreams.

Life Lessons:
— Stay passionate and on purpose.
— Empower yourself to excel even if no one is around to encourage you.
— Pray about everything—and worry about nothing.
— It is okay to admit that you need help.
— Be purposeful in your passion and passionate about your purpose.

W – WISDOM

Have you ever tried to solve a problem, made a mess, and *then* asked God for help? Have you ever said or thought, "I do not want to bother Jesus with this little task; I can do this on my own"?

Wisdom is the principal thing; therefore get wisdom: and with all thy getting get understanding.

—Proverbs 4:7 KJV

No matter the size of the issue or how bad the problem may be, God wants us to seek *Him* first. That is wisdom.

But seek ye first the kingdom of God, and his righteousness; and all these things shall be added unto you.

—Matthew 6:33 KJV

When you seek wisdom in all things, life can be so much easier. I have not always asked God before I made a move, but I have learned that when I seek God first and then wait for the answer, He moves in amazing ways and saves me time and money. I have less mess.

Seeking God is a crucial first step to being effective in life. Listening for an answer is the crucial next step. What may be a chore, like purchasing a tire, is simple to God. When my tire had to be replaced, I took the tire to two places, and I called one store. The first store told me I definitely needed to replace the tire. The tire could not be plugged or repaired. The tire place could order a tire. I called another place, and they had the best price but they also had to order the tire. I sought God for guidance. After seeking God, I was directed to the second company. I had to purchase a new tire, but the discount made this tire company the best choice.

I could have gone to several places and wasted more time, but after seeking God, not only did I spend my time wisely, but I got a better deal. Using wisdom in all tasks, no matter the size, can yield results you did not expect.

As you pray in the morning before starting your day, seek God for wisdom in every area. Ask God to grant you wisdom to:
— Prioritize your day
— Make healthy food choices
— Choose the right outfit
— Spend your money wisely

Life Lesson:
— Seek wisdom in all things and get understanding.

X - X-ING OUT FEAR

For God hath not given us the spirit of fear; but of power, and of love, and of a sound mind.

—2 Timothy 1:7 KJV

For ye have not received the spirit of bondage again to fear; but ye have received the Spirit of adoption, whereby we cry, Abba, Father.

—Romans 8:15 KJV

If God has not given us the spirit of fear or bondage, but of *power*, of *love*, and of a *sound mind*, then why do we allow fear to paralyze us, hinder us, weaken us, and prevent us from accomplishing all God has for us?

A few common fears include:
- Fear of public speaking
- Fear of making mistakes
- Fear of being closed in
- Fear of heights
- Fear of flying
- Fear of loving again
- Fear of what people may think
- Fear of the unknown
- Fear for your kids
- Fear you are not good enough
- Fear of failure
- Fear of success

If we stopped focusing on the fear of the thing and focus on the power the Creator has given us for His purpose, then we could accomplish all things through His strength.

> *Ask, and it shall be given to you; seek, and ye shall find; knock, and it shall be opened unto you: For every one that asketh receiveth; and he that seeketh findeth; and to him that knocketh it shall be opened.*
>
> —Matthew 7: 7–8 KJV

If our heavenly Father wants to give us good gifts, we cannot continue to walk in fear and be afraid. We must walk in power, love and a sound mind.

I want everything the heavenly Father has for me. I am expecting favor to chase me down! I am believing God that I will find favor not only with Him but with man, as well.

> *So shalt thou find favour and good understanding in the sight of God and man.*
>
> —Proverbs 3:4 KJV

I want supernatural favor. Supernatural favor and grace are synonymous in the New Testament. Natural favor can be earned, but supernatural favor is a gift.

I have obtained supernatural favor with loans for my car, my house, and more. I went expecting and believing God for it without doubt, and God granted me the gift. Let's spend more time asking, seeking, and knocking for *supernatural favor* and spend less time focusing on fear. I am confident the good gifts God wants to give us cannot be earned, but God has expectations of us in all things.

When fear starts to creep in, learn to call on the name of Jesus repeatedly until your spirit calms. Trust me, it works, and your accomplishments, not your fears or anxieties, will become your driving force.

Life Lessons:
— Release your fears and ask God to help you accomplish your goals. Ask God for a heart of faith to loose the shackles that have held you in bondage. Trust God for that shift and walk in the newness.
— Every time fear rears its ugly head, ask God to give you strength to overcome it.
— Remember, you can do all things through Christ.

Y - YES IS COMING

It is mind-blowing when "no" turns into "yes" because nobody knows everything you had to endure to get there. They do not see that your hands are up praising because you have tried door after door and watched the list of "no's" get longer and longer. I understand the frustration, disappointment, bitterness, and anger. Everyone around you is receiving a blessing, and you appear to be stuck.

> *Trust in the LORD with all thine heart; and lean not unto thine own understanding. In all thy ways acknowledge him, and he shall direct thy paths.*
>
> —Proverbs 3: 5–6 KJV

In 2014, I was two weeks away from closing on my house when the bank decided I was no longer an ideal candidate for them. I had paid my down payment. I had gotten the inspection. I was excited. I was lining up the movers and utilities. I had even given the mortgage representative a client, who had purchased her house shortly before I was scheduled to close. Her loan moved quickly, and she got her house. Meanwhile, the same bank was giving me a hard time because most of my income was derived from self-employment.

I had gone through a lot after the bankruptcy, and I needed a mortgage program that worked with self-employed and consulting professionals. The program I had gave me the runaround for six years. I was determined to own another home. My friends joked that I had the patience of Job.

The bank came back and indicated they would not be able to lend me the money. They felt that I might not have a job after the election if Trump won. Were they serious? Did they really say that to my face? I had a hard time with this perspective. I needed a lot of prayer and intercession because I was angry, disappointed, and frustrated. Actually, I was downright mad, and my attitude had to be adjusted because the bank was not trying to give me back my hard-earned money for the inspection or the down payment. I had to go to God seeking a miracle because I needed that money for a down payment with another lender.

I accepted that God does not make mistakes. I was reminded that God could have been protecting me from something bad I currently could not see, and so I focused on being grateful. Shortly thereafter, God shifted the process completely. I got a new Realtor and a new lender, and I went from looking at single-family homes to a townhouse. I had initially resisted the idea of a townhouse. It was just not in my plan. However, once I stopped fighting the process, God blew my mind. I got my home and a super deal.

I was doing well and was ready to pursue a business loan. As you know, when you are purchasing a house, you cannot obtain any other loans until the mortgage loan is completed and filed. It appeared the greater the levels, the bigger the devils. The lenders I had been confident would approve my loan called to say my loan was denied. Several lenders said my business had grown too quickly. I attributed it to the increase of commercial business and the opportunity I had had at the White House. God had shifted me to another place in my business prior to my White House experience, so I was already starting to operate in overflow on paper, you see, and I was waiting for my bank account to catch up. I needed to have a percentage of funds in my account to accommodate the projects that were coming through the pipeline.

When God gives you the vision, He has already made the provision. Eventually, I stopped focusing on the business loan and started trying to get my SUV instead. Then, in 2017, I received the business loan. I was leery, but I did it. I went for the loan with a backup plan to turn it around quickly and pay it off. The loan was not quite what I wanted, but I thought I needed it at the time. Sometimes, though, we can become too anxious. I soon realized I made a big mistake.

God had allowed me to see where I went ahead of Him, and now He was showing me His ways and making my crooked places straight. God turned it around and released a greater blessing than I had ever imagined. God paid off the previous loan and gave me favor to get out of debt. I had to come back to God for help because I did not wait and seek Him more! He is making me debt-free!

For a dream cometh through the multitude of business; and a fool's voice is known by multitude of words.

—Ecclesiastes 5:3 KJV

Life Lessons:
— Wait on the Lord!
— Be anxious for nothing!
— You have won! This is your *"winning season"*!

Z - ZEALOUS FOR GOD

I am grateful to God for pushing me to open up and be vulnerable with the hope that it may help others. I am zealous for my heavenly Father.

God has shown me so much grace and mercy, and I owe my all to Him. I have been set free, and freedom is a wonderful thing. I do not understand many things, but I am grateful, committed, devoted, and eager to serve God differently. I realize God has covered me in so many things and at so many times that they are too numerous to name. As I have sung so many times, if I had ten thousand tongues, I could not praise God enough for His goodness and mercy toward me!

I pray you will be set free. I pray you will grow and mature as a godly man or woman. We are not perfect, yet we serve a perfect God who is all-knowing, omnipotent, and omnipresent! He is the God of *all* the earth. I am grateful that God continues to perfect what He loves, and that sooner or later, things will turn in your favor. Hold on! Do not give up! This is your time to walk into your destiny, even if you are afraid, by trusting and relying completely on the promises of God!

Remember, you serve an AWESOME GOD!

He sits high, looks low, and has never forgotten about you! Believe God for *supernatural favor*!

One of my favorite books and prayers that will change your life and bless you tremendously is *The Prayer of Jabez*:

> "And _____(insert your name) called on the God of Israel saying, 'Oh, that You would bless me indeed, and enlarge my territory, that your hand would be with me, and that You would

keep me from evil, that I may not cause pain.' So God granted __ (insert your name) what he/she requested, just like He did for Jabez." In Jesus' name, amen!

Even when I *walked afraid,* God covered me. I trust I am covered by the *blood*! You, too, are covered by the *blood*!

Since the day we heard these things about you, we have continued praying for you. This is what we pray: that God will make you completely sure of what he wants by giving you all the wisdom and spiritual understanding you need; that this will help you live in a way that brings honor to the Lord and pleases him in every way; that your life will produce good works of every kind and that you will grow in your knowledge of God; that God will strengthen you with his own great power, so that you will be patient and not give up when troubles come. Then you will be happy and give thanks to the Father. He has made you able to have what he has promised to give all his holy people, who live in the light. God made us free from the power of darkness. And he brought us into the kingdom of his dear Son. The Son paid the price to make us free. In him we have forgiveness of our sins.

—Colossians 1:9–14 ERV

NOW I KNOW

Sometimes the ending does not look like you expected regarding the things you have prayed about, but God says, "It is done!" You may still be looking for the fireworks, only to realize you are missing a great celebration. You may still be waiting for something tangible and physical to occur to prove that it is done. Yes, you imagined it happening a certain way, but God said our ways are not like His ways. His ways are higher than our ways, and His supernatural blessings and favor says it is done, but it may not have lined up in the natural yet. So, what will you do? Whose report will you believe?

I will believe the report of the Lord. Keep praising like it is already done, because it is, and the manifestation will line up with the Word. People are going to think you are crazy. So what? Are they your provider?

God took me through a financial holding pattern during which things were held up. I could see those things that were supposed to happen in the physical, but they were delayed or pending. I was going through a birthing process. As uncomfortable as the process was, I had to go through it. It was not my will but His will that had to be done. I surrounded myself with people who were just as crazy as I am, who believe God can and has done a supernatural thing that man cannot explain. I have friends who are witnesses to what God can do with a person's finances. They are just other crazy people like me who believe God when He says, "*All things are possible for the one who believes!*" (Mark 9:23 ERV).

During the birthing process, your emotions are crazy, your body is tripping, you have anxiety and sleepless nights, and people give you bad advice. They may say you are having a girl when

God told you it is a boy or that you are going to have the baby soon when you know you have three more weeks before God delivers. Whose report do you believe?

Find the craziest friend you know who has witnessed firsthand the miracles of God, and pray, shout, and praise God together until that thing you have been praying for manifests in the natural. If others call you crazy, tell them you are crazy in love with Jesus and you know what God told you!

I will admit, the waiting process can be painful. I was fasting, praying, and seeing God purge people and things right before my eyes. My utilities were turned off, the bank was threatening me, and every account I had was overdrawn. I turned down my plate and left it down. The enemy was trying to make me abort my baby. I still tried to pay my tithes and do what I could because I knew God wanted to see what I would do with the little I had. I moved my feet with praise! Remember, God is waiting to see if we are going to keep complaining and whining, or if we will keep moving forward. Give God something to work with until He tells you to be still and stand. I knew it was part of the process. I was seeking God for answers. This was a hard test that I had to pass! I asked God, "What lesson am I supposed to learn? What am I doing wrong or not understanding, because this feels like a wilderness experience." There were times when God did not respond. At other times, God said, "I want to see how much you really trust Me."

God is birthing something greater out of you. All you have been through was to test your faith. Will you trust God with or without? Will you praise Him with little or much? When people discredit you and talk about you, will you still trust God, even though it hurts to the core? When people who can help you choose not to, are you going to still trust Him? If He blocks that person from helping you, will you get angry and have a bad attitude, or will you keep trusting God?

During this birthing process, God kept putting me in a place where I still had to pour into others when I just wanted to sit back and mind my own business. I wanted a complaining session. I just wanted someone to hear my story and be selfish for a change. When you empower everyone else and speak of empowerment on your radio show, God may very well send a word to tell you to empower yourself just like you do everyone else. You are baffled, but God knows everything! God does not want anyone to get in the way of His plan, including you. He wants you to rely completely on Him. God is a jealous God. He is your Provider! No one but Him will take the credit of saving you, providing for you, and giving you supernatural blessings and favor. If the answer is "no" from others, God wants you to depend and rely completely on Him for the "yes."

When my "yes" came, it was mind blowing! All the praying and believing God in the supernatural for blessings and favor, miracles, signs, and wonders finally had manifested in the natural. These were blessings that only God could provide! God wants us to dream big and stop asking for temporary "quick fixes" when He wants to give us long-term solutions. I started believing God for crazy-big things with no limitations. We have to stop limiting God. I believe God for a car that is paid in full, a mortgage that is paid off, a business that is restored, a husband on the way, healing for me and my family, and wholeness and soul salvation for family and extended family members. Yes, I want to be made whole. No more small thinking! I am asking big, dreaming big, and seeking a mindset shift like never before!

The revelation has blown my mind. Debts are being cancelled and wiped out. Miraculous blessings and favor are overflowing. God says, "It is done!" I am running toward the revelation of the manifestation as He continues to move.

I encourage you not to stop believing and asking. Dream big! Trust the process. It will hurt. It will pierce you. You will be challenged, but the reward is worth it. God will remove people—

some whom you did not believe would hurt you and others whom you suspected and God confirmed—so do not be surprised by His process. God will reveal *you* to you so He can clean you up, and it will be worth it! You will be purged and stretched, but you will come out as pure gold for His glory. Stay the course until it is time. Do everything you can to gird yourself with the Word.

There may be times when you cannot hear God. You block the distractions, and nothing happens. You get frustrated, wanting to hear from God. When the thing you have been waiting for is about to be released, you may become really anxious. You are about to reach another level in God. You may become really uncomfortable and unable to sleep. How you deal with people and things seems different, and you may even be short-tempered at times.

You just want the baby out. You are focused on giving birth. You know this labor pain is unbearable, and the false warnings are causing you to be in a state of frustration, up one day and down the next, but you are determined to keep going and not push before it is time. You know you cannot fix it, so you stop thinking about it and learn to just let God blow your mind.

You have the baby's room ready. What was meant to abort the baby cannot stop what God is doing. Soon, you will feel the shift and know it is time. You can feel God! You have been waiting for this time and this labor. And when it is time to push, you give it all you have, because you have been waiting for so long. Birth it! Birth it! Birth it!

No devil in hell can take what God has for you. Knowing that gives a peace that surpasses all understanding. Ready yourself to welcome your miracle. Stand in awe of Him. *Great is Thy faithfulness!*

> *"Come to me all of you who are tired from the heavy burden you have been forced to carry. I will give you rest. Accept my teaching. Learn from me. I am gentle and humble in spirit. And you will be able to get some rest.*

Yes, the teaching that I ask you to accept is easy. The load I give you to carry is light."

—Matthew 11:28–30 ERV

And at that point, the butterfly left the cocoon, and she is now soaring.

WALKING AFRAID ACTION BOOK

A 30-DAY JOURNEY TO FIND THE COURAGE TO ACT

I hope you have completed the reading of *Walking Afraid* and have experienced another level of vulnerability toward your healing that will kick you forward into your next best life. This workbook requires you to be truly vulnerable and open to the true feelings, disappointments, and frustrations that have hindered you.

As I was willing to be vulnerable in order to receive the healing I needed, I hope you will allow yourself to truly recognize those things that are keeping you from your next level. You must be completely honest with your feelings and seek God to heal those hurt places. Understand that being vulnerable to other people is so much different from being vulnerable to God. God will protect you, guide you, and direct you.

God is a safe place. He always wants the best for you. Other people may pretend to want what is best for you and try to help, but it is when you are truly at your most broken state that God can heal you.

To receive complete wholeness and healing, to grow beyond procrastination and be free, complete the action items in this workbook with your true heart.

Before getting started, make the decision to put it all on the table. Stop sugar-coating and dancing around how you feel. This place is where you can be free. Are you willing to do whatever it takes this time to forgive and to let go, which includes forgiving yourself? Be set free from the relationships that crushed you, the hurt in a ministry that turned you from the church, the disappointments at work or in a position you worked for but did not get, and the pain from people who talked and lied about you. Be set free from the bad business opportunity, the bad business loan, the bad partnership, or the financial issues that have kept you up and caused anxiety (whether you created it or God allowed it). Be set free from the strongholds, soul ties, generational curses, and health issues that were said to be terminal and caused you to be barren and angry. Be honest about what you truly need. Seek God with your whole heart so you can graduate into the life God intended for you to live.

Come soar with me and complete your journey. You have books to write, businesses to manage, and your own stories to share. People are waiting on you, and you must be willing to be broken and healed to receive everything God has for you. Let's go!

A-AMAZING GOD
DAY 1

Life Lessons:
— *God is amazing!* He continues to turn our brokenness into wholeness only if we are willing to trust Him and let go.
— Start with acknowledging your past and the people and things that continue to hold you hostage from moving forward, then seek God for wisdom.

Actions:
Identify three times in your past when, through the pain, you saw God's *awesome* power prevail! I know you have more, but let's start with three.

_____

_____

_____

_____

_____

After God transformed you, the situation, and/or the other person, what did you do next? Have you learned to trust more? Did you thank God for showing you yourself?

_____

_____

_____

_____

_____

Write down a few ways in which you are thankful and grateful for the hand of God in your life.

_____

_____

_____

_____

_____

Prayer/Scripture:
God, help me to be consistent in my walk with You so I may receive wholeness like You desire me to have. I pray for divine wisdom to grow past the circle that has kept me bound. I am seeking You for new mercies. In Jesus' name, amen!

B-BETTER AND BETTER
DAY 2

Life Lessons:
— You are not alone—no matter how you feel and regardless of who has left you. God has never left you, and He is all that matters. You may wonder how you can be so confident when life is painting a different picture. You must not look at your circumstances, but turn to the only true God of this universe, who made everything, including me and you. I challenge you to trust Him more than you did yesterday. How about giving God a high-five for keeping you this far? You may be surprised at how He responds. Trust Him more.
— Ask for *big* things and expect *big* things!
— Keep pouring out, and He will keep pouring in! Your living is not in vain!
— For every "no," a "*yes*" is coming! Expect it!
— Remember, some people will only serve a short time and purpose in your life; do not stop their departure. Your next steps and your growth may not include them. Do not resist the change.
— Trust the process! Celebrate where you are going!

Actions:
What life lessons have made you bitter instead of better?

_____

_____

_____

_____

_____

What would you change to stop the cycle you are in and why? Is forgiveness part of your resolution to healing?

_____

_____

_____

_____

_____

Prayer/Scripture:

> *Be strong and be brave. Don't be afraid of those people because the LORD your God is with you. He will not fail you or leave you.*
>
> —Deuteronomy 31:6 ERV

C - CONFRONTING THE PAST
DAY 3

Life Lessons:
— There is purpose in your pain. Depend on the Lord. Trust in Him, and He will heal you!
— What was meant to kill you only makes you better.
— Change how you look at a bad situation and see the lesson therein.
— Learn to leap for joy and watch God restore you!

Actions:
What life-changing situation has made you question its purpose in your life?

_____
_____
_____
_____
_____

Have you moved past the situation, or are you still struggling? Why or why not?

_____

_____

_____

_____

_____

What three things can you do to help yourself move forward?

_____

_____

_____

_____

_____

Prayer/Scripture:

> *Delight thyself also in the L*ORD*; and he shall give thee the desires of thine heart. Commit thy way unto the L*ORD*; trust also in him; and he shall bring it to pass.*
>
> —Psalm 37:4–5 KJV

D - DETERMINATION, DISAPPOINTMENT, AND DISCERNMENT
DAY 4

Life Lessons:
— Learn to *wait* with expectancy.
— Wait with a grateful heart and the right spirit. God is watching your responses to situations.
— Let God's voice overpower the other voices. When the delay comes—and it will—ask God to reveal to you the lesson(s) you are supposed to learn.

Actions:
How are you waiting? Circle all that apply.

Patiently

Anxiously

Angrily

Bitterly

With anticipation and/or with expectation

What three things have you learned about yourself during the waiting process? What is God saying that He wants you to do to grow past these things?

_____

_____

_____

_____

_____

_____

_____

_____

_____

_____

_____

_____

_____

Prayer/Scripture:

> *And whatsoever ye do, do it heartily, as to the Lord, and not unto men; knowing that of the Lord ye shall receive the reward of the inheritance: for ye serve the Lord Christ.*
>
> —Colossians 3:23–24 KJV

E - EMPOWERED TO EXCEL
DAY 5

Life Lessons:
- There is nothing too hard or impossible for God. If God said it, then it is done.
- Do not give up on your dream. Praise God through the storm and the distractions.
- A dream deferred is not a dream denied. Although it may tarry, wait with great expectation for it to come to pass.
- A delay is not a denial. Seek God for the next step.
- God can turn water into wine and cause two fish and five loaves of bread to feed thousands. Trust Him to change your situation.

Actions:
Are you experiencing the loss of something or someone? How are you feeling? Seek God for healing and for how to move forward.

_____

_____

_____

_____

_____

Are you asking God about the desires of your heart with the correct attitude?

Yes_____ No_____

If not, what do you need to do differently?

_____

_____

_____

_____

_____

What is the lesson you need to learn?

_____

_____

_____

_____

_____

Prayer/Scripture:

> *God is not a man that he should lie, neither the son of man, that he should repent: hath he said, and shall he not do it? or hath he spoken, and shall he not make it good?*
>
> —Numbers 23:19 KJV

F- FORGIVENESS
DAY 6

Life Lessons:
— Do not let FEAR (False Evidence Appearing Real) hinder God's plan.
— Obedience is better than sacrifice.
— God honors our sacrifice when our hearts are right and pure.
— Serve the Lord with fear and trembling (Psalm 2:11).
— Forgiveness is not always about the other person. When you forgive, you free *yourself*.

Actions:
Whom do you need to forgive? Why?

_____
_____
_____
_____
_____

Have you forgiven yourself?

Yes_____ No_____

You can start now.

_____
_____
_____
_____

_____

Write a letter to each person you need to forgive and decide whether or not you want to mail them. Regardless, make sure you have released it to God.

_____
_____
_____
_____
_____

Prayer/Scripture:

> *The fear of the LORD prolongeth days; but the years of the wicked shall be shortened.*
>
> —Proverbs 10:27 KJV

> *The LORD All-Powerful is the one you should fear. He is the one you should respect. He is the one who should frighten you.*
>
> —Isaiah 8:13 ERV

G - GOD, WHAT ARE YOU DOING?
DAY 7

Life Lessons:
— Be still and listen for God's voice.
— Things happen; do not dwell on what you cannot control.
— Discernment is a blessing.

Actions:
Have you ever had a "*God, seriously?*" moment in your life?

_____

_____

_____

_____

_____

_____

_____

_____

Prayer/Scripture:

Don't worry about anything, but pray and ask God for everything you need, always giving thanks for what you have. And because you belong to Christ Jesus, God's peace will stand guard over all your thoughts and feelings. His peace can do this far better than our human minds.

—Philippians 4:5–7 ERV

H - HIDDEN IN PLAIN SIGHT
DAY 8

Life Lessons:
— You have been hidden in plain sight for God to reveal who you are in His timing.
— Stay focused on God's Word.
— Do not get caught up in distractions.
— The process is necessary.
— Chaos is sometimes necessary; it has a purpose.
— You are running with the horses, not the footman.
— Remember the *Big Reveal*.

Actions:
What are you overlooking that perhaps has gotten you off track?

_____
_____
_____
_____
_____

Are the things necessary for your growth, or do you need to just take care of these things so you can move forward?

_____

_____

_____

_____

_____

Prayer/Scripture:
Father God, identify to the reader those things that have gotten them off track from Your plan. Give the person clarity and strength as You guide them to move forward, knowing Your master plan is greater and unlike any other. Whatever they are missing, restore and refuel their soul. In Jesus' name, amen!

I - ISSUE OF BLOOD
DAY 9

Life Lessons:
— Take care of *you* first.
— Do not sacrifice your health to the point of neglect.
— Take the time to rest and listen to your body.
— Put your mask on first before you put on or assist others with their masks.
— Let God's desire to make you whole be more important than your desire just to be healed.
— Rest in the arms of the Lord so that He can guide and direct you to your next.

Actions:
Have you ever sacrificed your health for others or to accomplish your dreams?

_____
_____
_____
_____
_____

What have you learned from sacrificing your health?

_____

_____

_____

_____

_____

What steps can you put in place to get back on track in one month, three months, six months?

_____

_____

_____

_____

_____

What is the difference between being physically healed and being made whole?

_____

_____

_____

_____

_____

What does "being made whole" look like for you right now? Ask God to make you whole.

_____
_____
_____
_____
_____

Prayer/Scripture:

Six days thou shalt work, but on the seventh day thou shalt rest: in earing time and in harvest thou shalt rest.

—Exodus 34:21 KJV

And he said unto him, Arise, go thy way: thy faith hath made thee whole.

—Luke 17:19 KJV

J - JUDGMENT AND JEALOUSY
DAY 10

Life Lessons:
- Cleanse me, Lord, and make me *whole*.
- Lord, take me and my mess, and make me into Your masterpiece.
- God, only You can judge. I take my hands off those situations that I have tried to control.
- Forgive me, Lord, for participating in gossip and judgment.
- Remove the envy and jealousy so I may operate fully in Your divine will.

Actions:
Identify any areas of judgment and jealousy in your life.

Judgment:

_____

_____

_____

_____

_____

Jealousy:

_____
_____
_____
_____
_____

Release these items to God, and ask Him to show you how to improve and purge them from your life. Listen for the answer, and write what God says to you.

_____
_____
_____
_____
_____
_____
_____
_____
_____

Prayer/Scripture:
Father God, create in us a clean heart and renew a right spirit in us, that we may be pleasing to You at all times. When the spirit of judgment and jealousy arise, let us be quick to release it to You. Purify us and make us whole. In Jesus' name, amen!

K - KNOCKING
DAY 11

Life Lessons:
— The more you study and meditate on the Word of God, the more you will build your spiritual life to hear God's voice.
— Stop fighting the process! If God has called you to do a task, give it your all. Show that you expect God to deliver on His promises by delivering on yours.
— Seek God for clarity and direction. It is okay to walk afraid; just trust that, in due time, God will give you understanding.
— Open yourself up and be willing to be available to His will and way. He will stretch you beyond your wildest dreams.

Actions:
What has God called you to do that you have not yet done? Ask God for forgiveness and to direct your steps.

_____
_____
_____
_____
_____

If you have not obtained clarity for what *God* is calling you to do, then take this time, *sit quietly* with paper and pencil in hand, ready to write what God has for you. Say, "Speak, Lord. Your servant hears."

_____

_____

_____

_____

_____

Prayer/Scripture:

Well done, thou good and faithful servant: thou hast been faithful over a few things, I will make thee ruler over many things.

—Matthew 25:21 KJV

L - LEARNING TO TRUST THE PROCESS
DAY 12

Life Lessons:
— Put your trust in God only.
— Wait for God to give you an answer.
— Stop talking and listen.
— Ask for wisdom.

Actions:
Walking afraid requires you to "trust the process" with *faith* and not fear! The process can be daunting, long, and fearful because of the unknown. What are you seeking God for that has taken a while, but yet you are still "trusting the process"?

_____

_____

_____

_____

_____

Have you been trusting with a positive attitude, or have you been on a roller coaster of emotion?

_____
_____
_____
_____
_____

If you have been trusting Him with the wrong attitude, seek God as to what you need to do next.

_____
_____
_____
_____
_____
_____
_____
_____
_____

Prayer/Scripture:

Wisdom is the principal thing; therefore get wisdom: and with all thy getting get understanding. Exalt her (wisdom), and she shall bring thee to honour, when thou dost embrace her.

—Proverbs 4:7 KJV

M - MINDSET OF MAKING IT
DAY 13

Life Lessons:
- Trust God more than yourself or other humans.
- When it gets hard—and it will—stay in constant communication with God.
- Remind God of His promises to you.
- Keep writing the vision and making it plain.
- Let God direct your path.
- There is nothing too hard for God. Keep this fact in the forefront of your mind and remind yourself as often as you can of almighty God's ability to *blow your mind!* "*Great is thy faithfulness*" (Lamentations 3:23b KJV).

Actions:
What things are blocking you from a "mindset of making it"?

_____
_____
_____
_____
_____

What steps can you take in the next six months to accomplish that thing your heart desires?

_____

_____

_____

_____

_____

Ask God for guidance and direction on your next steps, identifying all concerns that have blocked you in the past.

_____

_____

_____

_____

_____

Prayer/Scripture:

> *"To whom much was given, to him much will be required."*
> —Luke 12:48b ESV

> *For great is thy mercy toward me: and thou hast delivered my soul from the lowest hell.*
> —Psalm 86:13 KJV

> *Write down what I show you. Write it clearly on a sign so that the message will be easy to read.*
> —Habakkuk 2:2 ERV

M - MINDSET OF MAKING IT
DAY 13

Life Lessons:
- Trust God more than yourself or other humans.
- When it gets hard—and it will—stay in constant communication with God.
- Remind God of His promises to you.
- Keep writing the vision and making it plain.
- Let God direct your path.
- There is nothing too hard for God. Keep this fact in the forefront of your mind and remind yourself as often as you can of almighty God's ability to *blow your mind!* "*Great is thy faithfulness*" (Lamentations 3:23b KJV).

Actions:
What things are blocking you from a "mindset of making it"?

_____

_____

_____

_____

_____

What steps can you take in the next six months to accomplish that thing your heart desires?

_____

_____

_____

_____

_____

Ask God for guidance and direction on your next steps, identifying all concerns that have blocked you in the past.

_____

_____

_____

_____

_____

Prayer/Scripture:

"To whom much was given, to him much will be required."

—Luke 12:48b ESV

For great is thy mercy toward me: and thou hast delivered my soul from the lowest hell.

—Psalm 86:13 KJV

Write down what I show you. Write it clearly on a sign so that the message will be easy to read.

—Habakkuk 2:2 ERV

N - NO MEANS NO!
DAY 14

Life Lessons:
— No.
— No, *no*, nope.
— No to cancer.
— No to struggling, lack, and debt.
— No to people pulling on you and using your weakness for their gain.
— No to a need for man's approval of your next level.
— No to walking in fear; keep *walking afraid*

Actions:
No more struggling with *no*. . . . List all the people and things craving your attention to which you need to say *no*.

_____

_____

_____

_____

_____

Now send an email, make a phone call, and/or cut the tie. This should be an immediate action.

_____
_____
_____
_____
_____

Prayer/Scripture:
Father God, I pray for the person who is reading this book and working through their action steps. I pray for a fresh anointing on them now to say "no" in the very hard places where they have said "yes" for so many years. I ask You to renew their faith in You. Remove procrastination and the lies that tell them they cannot accomplish the dreams and desires You have placed in them. Remove any distractions that have kept them bound. This is a new walk. Lord, begin to open doors to new opportunities before they finish this book, and let them complete this plan with You. In Jesus' name, amen!

O - OPEN TO GOD'S WILL
DAY 15

Life Lessons:
— If it did not work your way, try God's way. He can never fail, and He does not disappoint!
— Great things are worth the wait.
— If you quit before the end of anything, you can always start over and go back! Force yourself to stay committed to the end.
— The greatest *reward* occurs toward the end of a thing. Press and push!
— Be just as dedicated to finishing something as you are to starting something new.
— Let God's perfect will be done.

Actions:
What have you started but have not finished?

_____
_____
_____
_____
_____

Are you willing to open yourself to follow God's will?

_____

_____

_____

_____

_____

What do you need to do to be fully committed to doing God's will?

_____

_____

_____

_____

_____

Prayer/Scripture:

> The Lord GOD says, "I will not delay any longer. If I say something will happen, it will happen!" This is what the Lord GOD said.
>
> —Ezekiel 12:28 ERV

P - PEACE OVERCOMES GUILT AND SHAME
DAY 16

Life Lessons:
— Nothing is too hard for God!
— Even in your pruning, you are being a blessing.
— Tell your story and free yourself.
— You are not crazy. What you went through was real, so do not let anyone tell you differently. Seek God to keep moving and growing into the best *you* ever!

Actions:
What people/things are affecting *your* peace?

_____

_____

_____

_____

_____

_____

_____

_____

_____

Have you released these items to God for good, or do you release them only to pick them back up again?

_____

_____

_____

_____

_____

Why are you still holding on to them when God gives you perfect peace?

_____

_____

_____

_____

Prayer/Scripture:

> *So be humble under God's powerful hand. Then he will lift you up when the right time comes. Give all your worries to him, because he cares for you. Control yourselves and be careful! The devil is your enemy, and he goes around like a roaring lion looking for someone to attack and eat. Refuse to follow the devil. Stand strong in your faith. You know that your brothers and sisters all over the world are having the same sufferings that you have. Yes, you will suffer for a short time. But after that, God will make everything right. He will make you strong. He will support you and keep you from falling. He is the God who gives all grace. He chose you to share in his glory in Christ. That glory will continue forever. All power is his forever. Amen.*
>
> —1 Peter 5:6–11 ERV

Q - QUESTIONING GOD
DAY 17

Life Lessons:
— He is an on-time God! Do not miss the blessing because you are blinded to your own way.
— Your greatest blessings look nothing like what you thought. Actually, none of your blessings looked like you imagined!

Actions:
There are things that just do not make sense. Have you been asking God for clarity?

_____
_____
_____
_____
_____

Even if God does not answer you, you must accept His will. Are you ready to accept God's will and persevere like never before? In due time, God could provide the answer. What will it take for you to *let go*?

_____

_____

_____

_____

_____

Prayer/Scripture:
Father God, send Your peace and comfort to us when we do not understand and life has thrown us a blow. We know You are too wise to make a mistake; therefore, we trust Your will and way. Continue to give us strength in the darkest of hours and light when we feel we are at the end of the tunnel. You are an all-knowing God, and nothing is too hard for You. We release all things to You, for You are a sovereign God who sits high and looks low. Thank You for the overflow of love and blessings! Thank You for Your grace and mercy! We count it all joy and accept Your divine will that if it is not well now, it will be well soon. In Jesus' name, amen!

R - RELATIONSHIPS AND REJECTION
DAY 18

Life Lessons:
— You may have been hurt, used, and abused in past relationships, but forgiveness is a must.
— Do not stay stuck because you refuse to let go.
— Remember, each relationship—good or bad—prepares you for what comes next in your life or the person you must help next.
— It is so true that some people are in your life for a season. You will know when that season is up.
— Take care of you! *Let go* of the old.
— The more you give, the more people will expect you to give. Ask God to show you how to give. It is not always money; it may be a prayer.
— You must determine if you *love you* enough to say "no" when you mentally and physically cannot give anymore. Do not allow guilt to force you to give in.
— Church hurt can make you turn away from God. Do not allow it to cause you to lose your faith and your relationship with God! Before changing churches, ask God whether you are to leave your church. You may be surprised by the answer.
— Check yourself. Sometimes it is *you*! Self-evaluation is a must.
— Stop trying to make old relationships fit into the new thing God is doing.

Actions:

Dig deep and ask yourself: What family members have you *not* forgiven?

_____
_____
_____
_____
_____

Do you remember what you are angry about? Is it worth it anymore to hold on to the offense?

_____
_____
_____
_____
_____

What do you need to do differently?

_____
_____
_____
_____
_____

Prayer/Scripture:

And no man putteth new wine into old bottles; else the new wine will burst the bottles, and be spilled, and the bottles shall perish.

—Luke 5:37 KJV

They fall in battle, totally defeated, but we survive and stand strong!

—Psalm 20:8 ERV

S - SUCCESFUL SERVANT
DAY 19

Life Lessons:
— Get a journal in which you can write out the lessons you've learned and to track your growth.
— Ask God for direction and listen for His answer, then move ahead based upon that answer.
— Ask God to send you a great prayer partner who will keep matters confidential.
— Ask God for *big* things, not just the small things.

Actions:
What are your top-five drivers to success?

_____
_____
_____
_____
_____

What factors are stopping you from being successful?

_____
_____
_____
_____
_____

Did you start writing in your journal?

_____
_____
_____
_____
_____

Did you ask God for your prayer partner?

_____
_____
_____
_____
_____

Prayer/Scripture:
Father God, give this reader Your definition of success *for his or her life. Show them how to practice "servant leadership" on the journey You have directed them to take. Father, when fear creeps upon them, bring them back to the Scriptures and a song that will refuel their faith. Thank You for the peace that surpasses all understanding and for meeting every one of their needs according to Your riches in glory. In Jesus' name, amen!*

T - TRIUMPH AT THE WHITE HOUSE
DAY 20

Life Lessons:
— You will either choose to accept the shift or stay stuck. You must choose. I choose to shift!
— Not everyone is for you.
— Man's rejection is not God's rejection; a delay is not a denial.
— Discernment is a beautiful thing when you listen and let God lead you.
— You never know who is watching you. Always put your best foot forward.

Actions:
Sometimes things do not work the first time. Are you still trying to do it the same way?

Yes_____ No_____

Ask God to send you the right help. Seek *wisdom* and *understanding* to do it *His way*. Now write what *the Father* told you to do next. Write the *vision, make it plain,* and stand on it.

_____
_____
_____
_____
_____

Prayer/Scripture:

Trust the LORD completely, and don't depend on your own knowledge. With every step you take, think about what he wants, and he will help you go the right way. Don't trust in your own wisdom, but fear and respect the LORD and stay away from evil. If you do this, it will be like a refreshing drink and medicine for your body.

—Proverbs 3:5–8 ERV

Honor the LORD with your wealth and the first part of your harvest. Then your barns will be full of grain, and your barrels will be overflowing with wine.

—Proverbs 3:9–10 ERV

U - UNDER GOD'S COVERING
DAY 21

Life Lessons:
— Today, tomorrow, this week, next week, this year, and the years to come, I will continue to make it a point to *walk afraid*!
— Ask God to surround you with people who will cry with you, laugh with you, and grow with you.
— You are *God's masterpiece*, uniquely made! Hear it again: You are *God's masterpiece*, uniquely made!

Actions:
What are you doing to change your thoughts, shifting your mind to the new? What actions do you need to take to live a life under the covering of God?

_____

_____

_____

_____

_____

_____

_____

_____

_____

_____

_____

_____

_____

_____

Prayer/Scripture:

No weapon that is formed against thee shall prosper; and every tongue that shall rise against thee in judgment thou shalt condemn. This is the heritage of the servants of the LORD, and their righteousness is of me, saith the LORD.

—Isaiah 54:17 KJV

V - VULNERABLE
DAY 22

Life Lessons:
— Stay *passionate* and on *purpose*.
— Empower yourself to *excel*, even if no one is around you to encourage you.
— Pray about everything—and worry about nothing.
— It is okay to admit that you need help.
— Be purposeful in your passion and passionate about your purpose.
— Open your hands to receive everything God has promised. A closed fist and a closed mind will leave you empty.
— *You are a winner!*

Actions:
Have you ever felt oppressed or depressed?

Yes_____ No_____

If yes, what are you doing about it? The first step is admitting that a problem exists. The next step is taking action to do something about it. Depression is real. You are not alone!

_____
_____
_____
_____
_____

Prayer/Scripture:

The effectual fervent prayer of a righteous man availeth much

—James 5:16b KJV

Happy is the man that findeth wisdom, and the man that getteth understanding. For the merchandise of it is better than the merchandise of silver, and the gain thereof than fine gold.

—Proverbs 3:13–14 KJV

W - WISDOM
DAY 23

Life Lessons:
— Seek wisdom in all things and get an understanding.
— As you pray in the morning before starting your day, ask God to grant you wisdom to help you in areas in order to:
  - Prioritize your day.
  - Make healthy food choices.
  - Choose the right outfit.
  - Spend money wisely.
  - Receive the life lessons that may come during the day and dismiss that which takes you off His course.

Actions:
Seek *wisdom* and *understanding* to do things God's way. Now write what God told you to do next. Write the vision and then stand on it.

_____

_____

_____

_____

_____

Prayer/Scripture:

My son [daughter], despise not the chastening of the Lord; *neither be weary of his correction: For whom the* Lord *loveth he correcteth; even as a father the son [daughter] in whom he delighteth.*

—Proverbs 3:11–12 kjv

But seek ye first the kingdom of God, and his righteousness; and all these things shall be added unto you.

—Matthew 6:33 kjv

Father God, I need a fresh anointing on the things You have called me to do. Show me how to be diligent in seeking You in all things, not just in my wants and desires or the temporary fixes, such as paying my utilities and this month's rent/mortgage, but in the big things (i.e., having my mortgage fully paid, building for my business, or gaining a mind-blowing promotion) and that which You have planned for me. I know all promotions and increases come from You. I choose to stop looking at man as my provider. I thank You in advance, Lord, for being my Jehovah-Jireh. In Jesus' name, amen!

X - X-ING OUT FEAR
DAY 24

Life Lessons:
— Release your fears and ask God to help you accomplish your goals. Ask God for a heart of faith to shake off the shackles that have held you in bondage. Trust God for that shift and walk in the newness it brings.
— Every time fear rears its ugly head, ask God to give you strength to overcome it.
— Remember: You can do all things through Christ.

Actions:
List your fears, large and small. Put the list before God to help you overcome each one.

_____
_____
_____
_____
_____
_____
_____
_____
_____
_____

Prayer/Scripture:

For God hath not given us the spirit of fear; but of power, and of love, and of a sound mind.

—2 Timothy 1:7 KJV

Be careful for nothing; but in every thing by prayer and supplication with thanksgiving let your requests be made known unto God.

—Philippians 4:6 KJV

For ye have not received the spirit of bondage again to fear; but ye have received the Spirit of adoption, whereby we cry, Abba, Father.

—Romans 8:15 KJV

And the peace of God, which passeth all understanding, shall keep your hearts and minds through Christ Jesus.

—Philippians 4:7 KJV

Y - YES IS COMING
DAY 25

Life Lessons:
— Wait on the Lord!
— Be anxious for nothing!
— *You have won!*
— Know that this is your "winning season"!

Actions:
Have you gotten over the disappointments, discouragements, and frustrations of life?

Yes_____ No_____

If you answered "yes," are you sure this is your true confession? Identify any areas you are still holding on to. Be true to yourself and God.

_____
_____
_____
_____
_____

Prayer/Scripture:

For the vision is yet for an appointed time, but at the end it shall speak, and not lie: though it tarry, wait for it; because it will surely come, it will not tarry.

—Habakkuk 2:3 KJV

For a dream cometh through the multitude of business: and a fool's voice is known by multitude of words.

—Ecclesiastes 5:3 KJV

Trust in the LORD with all thine heart; and lean not unto thine own understanding. In all thy ways acknowledge him, and he shall direct thy paths.

—Proverbs 3:5–6 KJV

Z - ZEALOUS FOR GOD
DAY 26

Life Lessons:
— Give thanks in all things big and small.
— Trust the process and praise your way through it, whatever your *it* may be.
— Remember: God is the same yesterday, today, and forever. He will never leave you nor forsake you.
— God is watching your response. Let go and let God transform you.
— He is an *awesome God*, and He loves you unconditionally.

Actions:
Take each letter in the alphabet and use it to describe God. It has been my pleasure to help you with your list, and I hope you will revisit it often. You have a lot to be thankful for, and so do I!

A - Awesome, Amazing,

_____

B - Beautiful

_____

C - Caring

_____

D -
E -
F -
G -
H -
I -
J -
K -
L -
M -
N -
O -
P -
Q -
R -
S -
T -
U -
V -
W -

X - _____

Y - _____

Z - Zealous

_____

Prayer/Scripture:
God has given us everything we need. He sits high and looks low, and He has never forgotten about you. Believe God for *supernatural favor* and *blessings*!

One of my favorite books and prayers, which will also forever change *your* life and bless *you* tremendously, is the Prayer of Jabez:

> *And _____ (insert your name) called on the God of Israel saying, "Oh that You would bless me indeed, and enlarge my territory, that your hand would be with me, and that You would keep me from evil, that I may not cause pain. So God granted _____ (insert your name) what he/she requested, just like He did for Jabez." In Jesus' name, Amen!*

Jesus has the power of God. And his power has given us everything we need to live a life devoted to God. We have these things because we know him. Jesus chose us by his glory and goodness, through which he also gave us the very great and rich gifts that he promised us. With these gifts you can share in being like God. And so you will escape the ruin that comes to people in the world because of the evil things they want. Because you have these blessings, do all you can to add to your life these things: to your faith add goodness; to your goodness add knowledge; to your knowledge add self-control; to your self-control add patience; to your patience add devotion to God; to your devotion add kindness toward your brothers and sisters in Christ, and to this kindness add love. If all these things are in you and growing, you will never fail to be useful to God. You will produce the kind of fruit that should come from your knowledge of our Lord Jesus Christ. But those who don't grow in these blessings are blind. They cannot see clearly what they have. They have forgotten that they were cleansed from their past sins. My brothers and sisters, God called you and chose you to be his. Do your best to live in a way that shows you really are God's called and chosen people. If you do all this, you will never fall. And you will be given a very great welcome into the kingdom of our Lord and Savior Jesus Christ, a kingdom that never ends. You already know these things. You are very strong in the truth you have. But I am always going to help you remember them. While I am still living here on earth, I think it is right for me to remind you of them. I know that I must soon leave this body. Our Lord Jesus Christ has shown me that. I will try my best to make sure you remember these things even after I am gone.

—2 Peter 1:3–15 ERV

NOW I KNOW
DAY 27

Life Lessons:
— I understand that I am not the author of my life. God owns and controls everything. As soon as I release my pain and thank God for taking the reins, I will begin to truly enjoy my best life ever.
— Never stop praising God! Praise God like the thing you have prayed for has already happened.
— Never give up!

Actions:
Receive your gift from God! Now that you are almost at the end of these thirty days of action, write a new letter to God giving thanks for the promises He has made. Write out the promises He has made to you, as well as your heart's desire. (There is extra room to complete your letter at the end of the book.) Not only are you writing the vision and making it plain, but you are thanking God for what He is about to release. God has made you brand-new, and you are walking in it—*walking afraid!*

_____

_____

_____

_____

_____

_____

_____

_____

_____

Prayer/Scripture:

Come to me all of you who are tired from the heavy burden you have been forced to carry. I will give you rest. Accept my teaching. Learn from me. I am gentle and humble in spirit. And you will be able to get some rest. Yes, the teaching that I ask you to accept is easy. The load I give you to carry is light.

—Matthew 11:28–30 ERV

Can anything separate us from Christ's love? Can trouble or problems or persecution separate us from his love? If we have no food or clothes or face danger or even death, will that separate us from his love? As the Scriptures say, "For you we are in danger of death all the time. People think we are worth no more than sheep to be killed." But in all these troubles we have complete victory through God, who has shown his love for us. Yes, I am sure that nothing can separate us from God's love—not death, life, angels, or ruling spirits. I am sure that nothing now, nothing in the future, no powers, nothing above us or nothing below us—nothing in the whole created world—will ever be able to separate us from the love God has shown us in Christ Jesus our Lord.

—Romans 8:35–39 ERV

PRAISE
DAY 28

Life Lessons:
— *Walk into your promises!*
— *Do not be afraid!*
— Your worst days are behind you.
— God has made all things new—just for *you*.
— You have been redeemed.
— Receive your reward, which has been given and cannot be earned!

Actions:
Sit quietly for thirty or more minutes. Ask God to give you a Scripture for the next level of your life. Write it out here and begin to repeat it to yourself daily.

_____

_____

_____

_____

_____

Ask God to give you a song to sing as well.

_____

_____

_____

_____

_____

Prayer/Scripture:

> *Since the day we heard these things about you, we have continued praying for you. This is what we pray: that God will make you completely sure of what he wants by giving you all the wisdom and spiritual understanding you need; that this will help you live in a way that brings honor to the Lord and pleases him in every way; that your life will produce good works of every kind and that you will grow in your knowledge of God; that God will strengthen you with his own great power, so that you will be patient and not give up when troubles come. Then you will be happy and give thanks to the Father. He has made you able to have what he has promised to give all his holy people, who live in the light. God has made us free from the power of darkness. And he brought us into the kingdom of his dear Son. The Son paid the price to make us free. In him we have forgiveness of our sins.*
>
> —Colossians 1:9–14 ERV

ENCOURAGE YOURSELF TO KEEP MOVING TOWARD THE PROMISES OF GOD
DAY 29

Life Lessons:
— Do not keep reliving your past. Choose to keep marching forward.
— If God said it, then believe it. If you believe it, then you will receive it. If you receive it, then you can achieve it.

Actions:
Sit quietly for thirty minutes or more. Reflect on this journey you have been on. Look at where you started and where you are now. You probably experienced a few trials along the way, but God continued to keep you. You did not know how you were going to make it, but you did. Keep pressing forward and celebrating your next phase. No matter how hard the days became, *you win*! Record your thoughts.

_____
_____
_____
_____
_____
_____
_____

_____

_____

_____

Father God, you are *amazing*! You brought us through, and we are experiencing *new beginnings*!

List eight things God brought you through during these past twenty-nine days, and do not despise the small things.

1. _____
2. _____
3. _____
4. _____
5. _____
6. _____
7. _____
8. _____

Prayer/Scripture:
Thank You, Lord, for one more sunny day! I am better for every trial. I may not see it now, but in due time I will understand. I trust You in all things. In Jesus' name, amen!

GIVE THANKS!
DAY 30

In every thing give thanks: for this is the will of God in Christ Jesus concerning you.

—1 Thessalonians 5:18

I am very proud of you! You have allowed God to stretch you, purge you, restore you, and rebuild you. This is a time for new beginnings in your life.

You have completed your first thirty-day action plan. Repeat the thirty-day challenge as often as you need to in order to get everything God has for you. You are free! What will you do now?

Actions:
Write a letter to yourself about how you feel. What is new for you? What did you learn? What was God's gift to you? What did He say to you?

_____
_____
_____
_____
_____
_____
_____
_____

_____
_____
_____
_____
_____
_____
_____

High-five yourself! This was not an easy task, but I hope you feel it was worth it.

Keep turning the pages. There is more of *you* to be released.

You do not look like what you have been through. *God* keeps refining you for *His* glory!

Prayer/Scripture:
May the blessings of overflow and abundance chase you down! In Jesus' name, amen!

> *"Remember ye not the former things, neither consider the things of old. Behold, I will do a new thing; now it shall spring forth; shall ye not know it? I will even make a way in the wilderness, and rivers in the desert. The beast of the field shall honour me, the dragons and the owls: because I give waters in the wilderness, and rivers in the desert, to give drink to my people, my chosen. This people have I formed for myself; they shall shew forth my praise."*
>
> Isaiah 43:18-21 KJV

PRAISE FOR CARNELA R. HILL

Carnela, let me be honest with you! In the last two months I've been purchasing books from different authors like . . . to give me that spark, motivation, the push I needed to keep moving forward but it didn't come to me until I read your book! OMG, every drop of hope I needed and wanted came from your truth, your words. I am beyond blessed right now. I'm filled with so much joy. This is what I've been needing. I love it, I love you, and I praise God for you!

I cried and I cried out to God to keep me moving beyond my fear! Affirmations! Just this month I have been reading and writing out affirmations!!! I was determined to read your book in twenty-four hours. It was like my life depended on it! Now I can really dig deep in the action plan! I'm so full of joy that the tears won't stop! God used me to give me my hope for right now–not tomorrow, but for right now! 🙏 Your words spoke to me! I found courage in your words. I related to so much to your story in the book, *Walking Afraid*! It is like this was meant just for me. Now I want it on Audible so I can listen to it every day! Thank you, Carnela, for being obedient to God! I can honestly say I have found the hope I've been searching for. Thank You, Jesus, for Carnela! The Lord uses His children to help and bless His children. 🙏 By the way, my life has changed this year! God has granted me one of my heart's desires. He allowed this amazing, loving man to find me and asked me to be his wife. I've been and still am on cloud nine. Just when I decided to just let God be my only husband, He blessed me with one. I will tell you all about him and our beautiful journey. 🌍 And there's a lot.

😊 It seems as if everything came about after reading *Walking Afraid*! Thank you, sis. Continue being obedient and following God's heart 🖤! I love you. 😊

— Lady L, consultant

When I think of Carnela, I think of someone who takes the next step enthusiastically regardless of the obstacles, as long as it is in alignment with the Word of God. Her faith is stronger than her fears. Through her actions, she inspires others—and myself—to do the same. Her standards are high, and that motivates others to be better when in her presence.

— Jimmy Davies,
Every.Black Family of Websites: www.Every.Black

I was amazed at Carnela's willingness to serve. She coordinated a staging for me that was supposed to be a simple twelve-by-twelve-foot space, but it ended up being a showroom in the middle of the mall that created quite a controversy from some of the anchor tenants. Carnela handled everything seamlessly. I didn't have to lift a finger or say one word. She elevated my game.

— Peggy Tatum,
publisher, *TCP Magazine*

When I think of Carnela Renée Hill, I think of courage, wisdom, and sophistication. Over the ten years of knowing Ms. Hill, she has served as my teacher and a trusted advisor, and she has become a lifelong friend. She has never ceased to amaze and inspire me, as she passionately pursues and conquers her professional goals with style and class. Her charismatic and distinguished personality is only magnified by her unmistakable faith in God. I am forever grateful for the privilege of knowing Ms. Hill and seeing her grow, while she continuously opens the eyes of many to new possibilities. Carnela Renée Hill truly embodies the definition of *phenomenal*.

— Danitra Rutherford,
owner of Nitra's Nook & The G.E.M Society

Carnela is one of my closest friends and my prayer partner, with whom I've shared many personal moments of adversity, perseverance, intercession, worship, and victorious triumph. Her enormous heart and love for others is the motivation and fervor for which she seeks to do the will of God. Many will be blessed by her amazing story and the testimony of how God has moved in her life. I'm so excited and overjoyed for my sister-friend!

— Shari Burton

I was blessed with Carnela's presence in my life during an extremely difficult time in both my personal and business life. She literally saved my life by being my prayer warrior and the discerning vessel God ordained her to be. I would recommend her book to anyone who needs a life-changing plan filled with Spirit-led teachings. My personal life now is "just as the doctor ordered," with a Spirit-filled gentleman in my life and my career abundantly blessed. As Carnela told me, God was about to *"blow my mind!!!"*

— Kimberly Vaughn,
the Glamour Girl of Comedy

When I first met the author of this book, she was truly "Walking Afraid." We had many conversations regarding her qualms and how to overcome them. Before I knew it, she was involved in multiple projects and taking on new adventures. It has been a pleasure to see her grow from a fearful skeptic to a woman who is not afraid to take on the world.

— Dr. LaMar Shannon,
director of education, Living Arts College

I love Carnela's perseverance. I have seen her plow through good and bad, and she keeps marching.

— JoAnne Lenart-Weary,
business coach

Walking Afraid is a must-read! It is riveting, captivating, and empowering. Carnela gives us insight into the power of perseverance, determination, and faith. Over the past twenty years, I've seen a transformation of great strength and extraordinary courage to overcome adversity.

— Bishop Cranford M. Davis,
senior pastor at A Fresh Anointed
Tabernacle of Deliverance

In her heart, Carnela never stopped believing that her passions and God's purpose were preparing her for the next phase of her journey. Our more-than-twenty-year friendship was, and still is, an opportunity to minister to each other through the good, bad, and indifferent. Her daily Facebook posts, both motivational and Spirit-driven, were as much of a challenge to herself as they were to the rest of the world to keep pushing! Her reflections on the past were only to measure the progress toward her destiny. Now I can clearly see God's hand at work in her life, and I believe *He* is well pleased with the results.

— Sonya Reid,
AKA soror and bona-fide friend

Carnela Hill is a classic beauty, full of wisdom and knowledge, whose strength allows her to conquer all her fears. She is faith-filled and focused. The vulnerability she displays in this book will inspire others to never give up on their dreams and goals.

— Kenya Wallace,
author of *Healthy, Happy, Whole*

Classy. Skillful. Poised. Encourager. Warrior. These are a few words to describe Carnela, a precious gift to the body of Christ. Carnela encouraged me at the most pivotal time of my life/being. I am forever grateful for her pushing me to go beyond what my eyes saw to connect with the vision God had for me. As God continues to connect our dots, let us continue to grow more in His wisdom, statutes, and grace. I am excited for Carnela, but even more blessed to take this journey with her into the next chapter of our lives. Stay in faith and receive all He has for you with humility and honor.

— Parris Solomon,
author of *She: Rare Essence of Beauty and Purpose*

REFERENCES

Kerr, B. *Depression Among Entrepreneurs is an Epidemic Nobody is Talking About*, October 26, 2015. Retrieved from https://thehustle.co.